Master Python

Without Prior Experience

Table of Contents

Introduction

Welcome to your journey with "Master Python Without Prior Experience"! This book is your comprehensive guide to learning Python programming from scratch. You'll start with the basics of programming and why Python is a great language to learn. You'll set up your Python environment and start coding in no time.

You'll delve into the core concepts of Python, including variables, data types, operators, control flow, and more. You'll explore Python's rich collection of data structures and learn how to define and use functions and modules.

You'll also learn about file handling in Python, including how to read from and write to files, and work with CSV and JSON files.

One of the key strengths of Python is its support for object-oriented programming (OOP), and you'll spend time understanding classes, objects, inheritance, polymorphism, and more.

Exception handling is a critical part of writing robust, error-free code, and you'll cover that too, including how to raise and handle exceptions.

To help you apply what you've learned, you'll work on practical Python projects that will give you hands-on experience with building a web scraper, creating a command-line tool, developing a GUI application, and working with APIs and data analysis.

Finally, you'll be introduced to the Python ecosystem and resources, including popular Python libraries and frameworks, package management, and where to find Python documentation and community support.

The appendices include a handy Python cheat sheet, additional practice problems, and a glossary of terms.

Chapter 1: Introduction to Programming and Python

Programming is a fascinating and powerful skill that allows you to create software, automate tasks, and solve complex problems. In today's digital age, programming has become increasingly important across various industries, from technology and finance to scientific research and creative fields. Whether you're interested in building websites, developing mobile applications, analyzing data, or creating games, programming opens up a world of possibilities.

This chapter will introduce you to the concept of programming and provide an overview of Python, one of the most popular and versatile programming languages. We'll explore the reasons for learning Python, its advantages, and the process of setting up your Python development environment.

1.1 What is Programming?

Programming is the process of writing instructions, known as code, for a computer to execute. These instructions are written in a programming language, which is a formal language designed to be understood by both humans and computers. Programming languages have their own syntax and rules, much like natural languages have grammar and vocabulary.

When you write a program, you essentially provide a series of step-by-step instructions that tell the computer how to perform a specific task or solve a particular problem. These instructions can range from simple calculations and data manipulation to complex algorithms and artificial intelligence applications.

Programming is a creative and problem-solving activity that requires logical thinking, attention to detail, and the ability to break down complex problems into smaller, manageable parts. It involves analyzing requirements, designing solutions, writing code, testing and debugging, and maintaining and updating existing programs.

1.2 Why Learn Python?

Python is a high-level, general-purpose programming language that was first released in 1991 by Guido van Rossum. It has gained immense popularity over the years due to its simplicity, readability, and versatility. Python is widely used in various domains, including web development, data analysis, machine learning, automation, and scientific computing.

Here are some compelling reasons to learn Python:

1. Easy to Learn: Python is known for its clear and concise syntax, making it relatively easy to learn, especially for beginners. Its simple and intuitive structure allows you to focus on the core concepts of programming without getting bogged down by complex language constructs.

2. Versatile: Python is a versatile language that can be used for a wide range of applications, from web development and data analysis to automation, scripting, and even game development. Its extensive standard library and numerous third-party libraries and frameworks make it a powerful tool for tackling diverse programming tasks.

3. Cross-Platform: Python is a cross-platform language, meaning that Python programs can run on various operating systems, including Windows, macOS, and Linux, without requiring significant modifications to the code.

4. Interpreted Language: Python is an interpreted language, which means that Python code is executed line by line without the need for a separate compilation step. This feature makes the development and testing process more efficient, as you can see the results of your code immediately.

5. Extensive Libraries and Frameworks: Python has a vast and growing ecosystem of libraries and frameworks that provide ready-to-use solutions for various tasks. Libraries like NumPy, Pandas, and Matplotlib are widely used for scientific computing and data analysis, while frameworks like Django and Flask are popular for web development.

6. Supportive Community: Python has a large and active community of developers, enthusiasts, and contributors. This community provides extensive documentation, tutorials, and forums where you can find help, share knowledge, and collaborate on projects.

7. High-Level Language: Python is a high-level language, which means it abstracts away many low-level details of computer hardware and operating systems. This abstraction allows developers to focus on solving problems rather than worrying about low-level implementation details.

8. Readability and Maintainability: Python's emphasis on readability and code organization promotes writing clean and maintainable code. Its use of whitespace indentation and clear syntax makes Python code easy to read and understand, even for those who are new to the language.

9. Rapid Prototyping: Python's simplicity and ease of use make it an excellent choice for rapid prototyping and quickly testing ideas. Its interactive shell (Python interpreter) allows you to experiment with code snippets and see the results instantly.

10. Scalability: Python can be used for small scripts or large-scale applications. Its modular design and extensive libraries make it easy to build and scale complex projects.

Whether you're a beginner or an experienced programmer, learning Python can open up a world of opportunities in various fields, from web development and data analysis to automation and scientific computing.

1.3 Setting Up Your Python Environment

Before you can start writing and running Python code, you need to set up your Python development environment. This involves installing Python itself and optionally setting up an Integrated Development Environment (IDE) or text editor to write and edit your code.

Installing Python

Python is available for various operating systems, including Windows, macOS, and Linux. You can download the latest version of Python from the official Python website (https://www.python.org/downloads/).

Follow these steps to install Python on your system:

1. Visit the Python downloads page (https://www.python.org/downloads/) and select the appropriate version for your operating system.
2. Run the installer and follow the on-screen instructions.
3. During the installation process, make sure to select the option to add Python to your system's PATH environment variable. This will allow you to run Python from the command line or terminal without specifying the full path to the Python executable.
4. After the installation is complete, open your command prompt or terminal and type `python --version`. If Python is installed correctly, you should see the version number displayed.

Setting Up an IDE or Text Editor

While you can write and run Python code using a simple text editor, an Integrated Development Environment (IDE) or a code editor with Python support can greatly enhance your coding experience. IDEs and code editors provide features like syntax highlighting, code completion, debugging tools, and project management, which can make writing and debugging Python code more efficient.

Here are some popular options for Python IDEs and code editors:

1. PyCharm: PyCharm is a powerful IDE developed by JetBrains specifically for Python development. It offers a wide range of features, including code completion, refactoring tools, debugging, and support for various Python frameworks and libraries. PyCharm is available in both a free Community Edition and a paid Professional Edition.

2. Visual Studio Code: Visual Studio Code (VS Code) is a popular, free, and open-source code editor developed by Microsoft. While not specifically designed for Python, it has excellent support for Python development through the Python extension. VS Code offers features like code completion, debugging, and integration with popular Python tools and libraries.

3. Sublime Text: Sublime Text is a lightweight and highly customizable text editor that supports Python development through various plugins and packages. It offers features like syntax highlighting, code completion, and a powerful search and replace functionality.

4. Atom: Atom is a free and open-source text editor developed by GitHub. It has a built-in package manager and a vast community of developers contributing packages and plugins, including those for Python development.

5. IDLE: IDLE (Integrated Development and Learning Environment) is a simple IDE that comes bundled with Python installations. It provides a basic code editor, a Python shell, and debugging tools. IDLE is a great option for beginners who want a lightweight and straightforward environment to start learning Python.

6. Jupyter Notebook: Jupyter Notebook is a web-based interactive computing environment that allows you to create and share documents that contain live code, visualizations, and narrative text. It is widely used in data science, scientific computing, and educational contexts.

When choosing an IDE or code editor, consider factors such as your personal preferences, the features you need, and the level of support for Python development. Many of these tools offer free versions or trials, so you can explore different options and choose the one that best suits your needs.

In the next chapter, we'll dive into the basics of Python programming, covering essential concepts like variables, data types, operators, and control flow statements. With your Python environment set up, you'll be ready to start writing and running your first Python programs.

Chapter 2: Python Basics

In this chapter, we'll dive into the fundamental building blocks of Python programming. Understanding these basics is crucial for writing effective and efficient code. We'll cover topics such as variables, data types, operators, expressions, user input and output, and control flow statements like conditionals and loops.

2.1 Variables and Data Types

Variables are containers used to store values in a program. They act as named placeholders that can hold different types of data. In Python, you don't need to explicitly declare the data type of a variable; the type is determined dynamically based on the value assigned to it.

Here's an example of creating and assigning values to variables in Python:

```python
age = 25
name = "Alice"
is_student = True
weight = 65.4
```

In the example above, `age` is an integer variable, `name` is a string variable, `is_student` is a boolean variable, and `weight` is a float variable.

Python supports several built-in data types, including:

1. **Integers (int):** Whole numbers, positive or negative, without decimal points. Examples: `42`, `-7`, `0`.

2. **Floating-point numbers (float):** Numbers with decimal points. Examples: `3.14`, `-0.75`, `6.022e23` (scientific notation).

3. **Strings (str):** Sequences of characters enclosed in single quotes (`'`), double quotes (`"`), or triple quotes (`'''`or `"""`for multi-line strings). Examples: `"Hello, World!"`, `'Python'`, `"""This is
a multi-line
string."""`

4. **Booleans (bool):** Logical values representing `True` or `False`.

5. **Lists (list):** Ordered collections of items, enclosed in square brackets (`[`and `]`). Lists can contain elements of different data types. Examples: `[1, 2, 3]`, `['apple', 'banana', 'cherry']`, `[True, False, True]`.

6. **Tuples (tuple):** Ordered, immutable collections of items, enclosed in parentheses (`(`and `)`). Tuples are similar to lists but cannot be modified after creation. Examples: `(1, 2, 3)`, `('a', 'b', 'c')`.

7. Dictionaries (dict): Unordered collections of key-value pairs, enclosed in curly braces (`{`and `}`). Each key in a dictionary must be unique and immutable (like strings or numbers). Examples: `{'name': 'Alice', 'age': 25}`, `{1: 'apple', 2: 'banana'}`.

8. Sets (set): Unordered collections of unique elements, enclosed in curly braces (`{`and `}`). Sets are useful for removing duplicates and performing mathematical operations like unions and intersections. Examples: `{1, 2, 3}`, `{'a', 'b', 'c'}`.

You can check the type of a variable using the `type()` function:

```python
print(type(25))      # Output: <class 'int'>
print(type(3.14))    # Output: <class 'float'>
print(type("Hello")) # Output: <class 'str'>
```

Python also supports type conversion functions like `int()`, `float()`, `str()`, `bool()`, `list()`, `tuple()`, `dict()`, and `set()` to convert values between different data types.

2.2 Operators and Expressions

Operators are symbols or keywords that perform specific operations on values or variables. Python supports various types of operators, including arithmetic, assignment, comparison, logical, bitwise, and more.

Arithmetic Operators

Arithmetic operators are used to perform mathematical operations on numeric values. Here are some common arithmetic operators:

- `+` (Addition): `2 + 3` evaluates to `5`
- `-` (Subtraction): `5 - 2` evaluates to `3`
- `*` (Multiplication): `3 * 4` evaluates to `12`
- `/` (Division): `10 / 2` evaluates to `5.0` (float division)
- `//` (Floor Division): `10 // 3` evaluates to `3` (integer division, rounding down)
- `%` (Modulus): `10 % 3` evaluates to `1` (remainder of division)
- `` (Exponentiation): `2  3` evaluates to `8` (2 raised to the power of 3)

Assignment Operators

Assignment operators are used to assign values to variables. The basic assignment operator is `=`:

```python
x = 5      # Assign the value 5 to the variable x
y = x + 3 # Assign the value 8 (5 + 3) to the variable y
```

Python also supports compound assignment operators that combine an arithmetic operation and an assignment:

- `+=`: `x += 3` is equivalent to `x = x + 3`
- `-=`: `x -= 2` is equivalent to `x = x - 2`
- `*=`: `x *= 4` is equivalent to `x = x * 4`
- `/=`: `x /= 2` is equivalent to `x = x / 2`
- `//=`: `x //= 3` is equivalent to `x = x // 3`
- `%=`: `x %= 2` is equivalent to `x = x % 2`
- `=`: `x = 3` is equivalent to `x = x  3`

Comparison Operators

Comparison operators are used to compare values and evaluate to a boolean result (`True` or `False`). Here are the common comparison operators:

- `==` (Equal to): `5 == 5` evaluates to `True`
- `!=` (Not equal to): `3 != 4` evaluates to `True`
- `>` (Greater than): `7 > 5` evaluates to `True`
- `<` (Less than): `2 < 9` evaluates to `True`
- `>=` (Greater than or equal to): `6 >= 6` evaluates to `True`
- `<=` (Less than or equal to): `4 <= 7` evaluates to `True`

Logical Operators

Logical operators are used to combine or negate boolean values. The three main logical operators are:

- `and`: Returns `True` if both operands are `True`, otherwise `False`. Example: `(5 > 3) and (2 < 7)` evaluates to `True`.
- `or`: Returns `True` if at least one operand is `True`, otherwise `False`. Example: `(5 > 7) or (3 < 2)` evaluates to `False`.
- `not`: Returns the opposite boolean value of the operand. Example: `not (5 > 3)` evaluates to `False`.

Bitwise Operators

Bitwise operators perform operations on individual bits of binary numbers. While they are not as commonly used as other operators, they can be useful in certain situations, such as low-level programming or working with binary data. Some common bitwise operators are:

- `&` (Bitwise AND)
- `|` (Bitwise OR)
- `^` (Bitwise XOR)
- `~` (Bitwise NOT)
- `<<` (Bitwise Left Shift)
- `>>` (Bitwise Right Shift)

Expressions

An expression is a combination of values, variables, operators, and function calls that produce a result. Expressions can be simple, like `2 + 3`, or more complex, like `(x 2 + y 2) 0.5`.

Here are some examples of expressions in Python:

```python
result = 5 + 3 * 2    # 11 (multiplication takes precedence over addition)
x = 10
y = 3
hypotenuse = (x  2 + y  2)  0.5  # 10.44... (using exponentiation and square root)
greeting = "Hello, " + "world!"  # "Hello, world!" (string concatenation)
is_even = 7 % 2 == 0  # False (modulus and comparison operators)
```

Expressions can be evaluated and their results can be stored in variables or used directly in other operations or function calls.

2.3 User Input and Output

In many programs, you'll need to interact with users by getting input from them or displaying output. Python provides built-in functions for handling user input and output.

Getting User Input

The `input()` function is used to get input from the user through the console or terminal. It accepts an optional string argument that serves as a prompt for the user:

```python
name = input("Enter your name: ")
print("Hello, " + name + "!")
```

In the example above, the `input()` function prompts the user with the message "Enter your name: " and waits for the user to enter a value. The entered value is then stored in the `name` variable.

Note that the `input()` function always returns a string value, regardless of the input type. If you need to work with numeric input, you'll need to convert the input string to the appropriate numeric type:

```python
age = int(input("Enter your age: "))
print("You are", age, "years old.")
```

Here, the `int()` function is used to convert the input string to an integer before storing it in the `age` variable.

Displaying Output

The `print()` function is used to display output to the console or terminal:

```python
print("Hello, World!")
```

The `print()` function can take multiple arguments, which will be printed with spaces in between:

```python
name = "Alice"
age = 25
print("My name is", name, "and I'm", age, "years old.")
```

This will output:

```
My name is Alice and I'm 25 years old.
```

You can also use string formatting or f-strings (Python 3.6+) to include variable values directly in the output string:

```python
name = "Bob"
age = 30
print(f"My name is {name} and I'm {age} years old.")
```

This will output:

```
My name is Bob and I'm 30 years old.
```

The `print()` function also provides additional options, such as customizing the separator between arguments (`sep=`) and the end character (`end=`):

```python
print("Hello", "World", sep=", ", end="!\n")
print("This is another line.")
```

This will output:

```
Hello, World!
This is another line.
```

In the example above, the `sep=", "` argument specifies that the arguments should be separated by a comma and a space, and the `end="!\n"` argument adds an exclamation mark and a newline character to the end of the output.

2.4 Control Flow (If-Else, Loops)

Control flow statements are used to control the order in which statements are executed in a program. Python provides several control flow constructs, including conditional statements (if-else) and loops (for and while).

Conditional Statements (If-Else)

Conditional statements allow you to execute different blocks of code based on certain conditions. The `if` statement is the most basic conditional statement in Python:

```python
age = 18

if age >= 18:
    print("You are an adult.")
else:
    print("You are a minor.")
```

In this example, the code inside the `if` block will be executed if the condition `age >= 18` is `True`. Otherwise, the code inside the `else` block will be executed.

You can also use the `elif` (short for "else if") statement to add additional conditions:

```python
grade = 85

if grade >= 90:
    print("You got an A.")
elif grade >= 80:
    print("You got a B.")
elif grade >= 70:
    print("You got a C.")
else:
    print("You need to improve.")
```

Here, the conditions are checked from top to bottom, and the first condition that evaluates to `True` will have its corresponding block executed. Once a block is executed, the control flow exits the conditional statement.

Loops

Loops are used to repeatedly execute a block of code. Python provides two main types of loops: `for` loops and `while` loops.

For Loops

The `for` loop is used to iterate over a sequence (such as a list, tuple, string, or range) or other iterable objects:

```python
fruits = ["apple", "banana", "cherry"]

for fruit in fruits:
    print(fruit)
```

This will output:

```
apple
banana
cherry
```

You can also use the `range()` function to generate a sequence of numbers:

```python
for i in range(5):
    print(i)
```

This will output:

```
0
1
2
3
4
```

The `range()` function generates a sequence of numbers starting from 0 by default, up to (but not including) the specified number. You can also provide additional arguments to `range()` to specify the start and step values:

```python
for i in range(2, 10, 2):
    print(i)
```

This will output:

```
2
4
6
8
```

In this example, the `range(2, 10, 2)` generates a sequence of numbers starting from 2, up to (but not including) 10, with a step size of 2.

While Loops

The `while` loop is used to repeatedly execute a block of code as long as a certain condition is `True`:

```python
count = 0

while count < 5:
    print(count)
    count += 1
```

This will output:

```
0
1
2
3
4
```

In this example, the loop will continue executing as long as `count` is less than 5. Inside the loop, we print the value of `count` and then increment it by 1.

You can also combine `break` and `continue` statements with loops to control their execution:

- `break` is used to exit the loop prematurely.
- `continue` is used to skip the current iteration and move to the next one.

```python
for i in range(10):
    if i == 5:
        break
    print(i)

print("Loop exited.")

for i in range(10):
    if i % 2 == 0:
        continue
    print(i)
```

This will output:

```
0
1
2
3
4
Loop exited.
1
3
5
7
9
```

In the first loop, when `i` becomes 5, the `break` statement is executed, and the loop exits prematurely. In the second loop, when `i` is even (divisible by 2 with no remainder), the `continue` statement is executed, and the current iteration is skipped.

Control flow statements are fundamental to writing powerful and flexible programs in Python. By combining conditional statements and loops, you can create complex logic and algorithms to solve a wide range of problems.

Exercise: Simple Calculator

Create a program that simulates a simple calculator. The program should prompt the user to enter two numbers and an operator (+, -, *, /). It should then perform the corresponding arithmetic operation and display the result.

Solution:

```python
print("Welcome to the Simple Calculator!")

num1 = float(input("Enter the first number: "))
```

```python
operator = input("Enter the operator (+, -, *, /): ")
num2 = float(input("Enter the second number: "))

if operator == "+":
    result = num1 + num2
elif operator == "-":
    result = num1 - num2
elif operator == "*":
    result = num1 * num2
elif operator == "/":
    if num2 != 0:
        result = num1 / num2
    else:
        print("Error: Division by zero!")
        result = None
else:
    print("Invalid operator!")
    result = None

if result is not None:
    print(f"{num1} {operator} {num2} = {result}")
```

Explanation:

1. The program prompts the user to enter the first number using input() and converts it to a float.
2. The program prompts the user to enter the operator (+, -, *, /) using input().
3. The program prompts the user to enter the second number using input() and converts it to a float.
4. The program uses an if-elif-else statement to perform the appropriate arithmetic operation based on the operator entered by the user.
5. If the operator is division (/) and the second number is zero, an error message is printed, and the result is set to None.
6. If the result is not None (i.e., a valid operation was performed), the program prints the result using an f-string.

Project: Leap Year Checker

Write a program that prompts the user to enter a year and checks whether it is a leap year or not. A leap year is a year that is divisible by 4, except for years that are divisible by 100 (which are not leap years), unless the year is also divisible by 400 (which are leap years).

Solution:

```python
year = int(input("Enter a year: "))

if year % 4 == 0:
    if year % 100 == 0:
        if year % 400 == 0:
            is_leap_year = True
        else:
            is_leap_year = False
```

```python
    else:
        is_leap_year = True
else:
    is_leap_year = False

if is_leap_year:
    print(f"{year} is a leap year.")
else:
    print(f"{year} is not a leap year.")
```

Explanation:

1. The program prompts the user to enter a year using input() and converts it to an int.
2. The program uses a nested if-elif-else statement to determine whether the year is a leap year or not, based on the following conditions:
   - If the year is divisible by 4, it might be a leap year.
   - If the year is divisible by 100, it is not a leap year, unless it is also divisible by 400.
   - If the year is divisible by 400, it is a leap year.
3. The program stores the result of the leap year check in the is_leap_year variable, which is a bool (True or False).
4. Finally, the program prints a message indicating whether the year is a leap year or not, using the value of the is_leap_year variable.

Chapter 3: Data Structures in Python

3.1 Lists

Lists are one of the most versatile and widely used data structures in Python. They are ordered collections of items, which can be of different data types. Lists are mutable, meaning you can add, remove, or modify elements after creating the list.

Creating Lists

Lists are created by enclosing items (elements) within square brackets `[]` and separating them by commas. Here are some examples of creating lists in Python:

```python
# Empty list
empty_list = []

# List of integers
numbers = [1, 2, 3, 4, 5]

# List of strings
names = ["Alice", "Bob", "Charlie"]

# List of mixed data types
mixed_list = [1, "apple", 3.14, True]
```

Accessing List Elements

You can access individual elements in a list using indexing. Indexing in Python starts from 0, so the first element has an index of 0, the second element has an index of 1, and so on.

```python
fruits = ["apple", "banana", "cherry"]

# Access the first element
print(fruits[0])  # Output: apple

# Access the second element
print(fruits[1])  # Output: banana

# Access the last element
print(fruits[-1])  # Output: cherry
```

Negative indices can be used to access elements from the end of the list. The index `-1` refers to the last element, `-2` refers to the second-to-last element, and so on.

You can also use slicing to access a range of elements in a list. The syntax is `list_name[start:stop:step]`, where `start` is the index to start from (inclusive), `stop` is the index to stop at (exclusive), and `step` is the step size (optional, defaults to 1).

```python
numbers = [1, 2, 3, 4, 5, 6, 7, 8, 9, 10]

# Slice from index 2 to index 6 (exclusive)
print(numbers[2:6])  # Output: [3, 4, 5, 6]

# Slice from the beginning to index 4 (exclusive)
print(numbers[:4])  # Output: [1, 2, 3, 4]

# Slice from index 6 to the end
print(numbers[6:])  # Output: [7, 8, 9, 10]

# Slice with a step size of 2
print(numbers[1:8:2])  # Output: [2, 4, 6, 8]
```

Modifying Lists

Lists are mutable, which means you can add, remove, or modify elements after creating the list.

Adding Elements

- `append(element)`: Adds an element to the end of the list.
- `insert(index, element)`: Inserts an element at the specified index.
- `extend(iterable)`: Adds the elements from an iterable (like another list) to the end of the list.

```python
fruits = ["apple", "banana"]

# Append an element
fruits.append("cherry")
print(fruits)  # Output: ['apple', 'banana', 'cherry']

# Insert an element at index 1
fruits.insert(1, "orange")
print(fruits)  # Output: ['apple', 'orange', 'banana', 'cherry']

# Extend the list with another list
more_fruits = ["mango", "kiwi"]
fruits.extend(more_fruits)
print(fruits)  # Output: ['apple', 'orange', 'banana', 'cherry', 'mango',
'kiwi']
```

Removing Elements

- `remove(element)`: Removes the first occurrence of the specified element from the list.
- `pop(index)`: Removes and returns the element at the specified index. If no index is provided, it removes and returns the last element.
- `clear()`: Removes all elements from the list.

```python
fruits = ["apple", "banana", "cherry", "banana"]

# Remove the first occurrence of "banana"
fruits.remove("banana")
print(fruits)  # Output: ['apple', 'cherry', 'banana']

# Remove and return the element at index 1
removed_fruit = fruits.pop(1)
print(removed_fruit)  # Output: 'cherry'
print(fruits)  # Output: ['apple', 'banana']

# Remove the last element
last_fruit = fruits.pop()
print(last_fruit)  # Output: 'banana'
print(fruits)  # Output: ['apple']

# Clear the list
fruits.clear()
print(fruits)  # Output: []
```

Modifying Elements

You can modify the elements in a list by assigning new values to specific indices.

```python
numbers = [1, 2, 3, 4, 5]

# Modify the element at index 2
numbers[2] = 10
print(numbers)  # Output: [1, 2, 10, 4, 5]

# Modify a range of elements using slicing
numbers[1:4] = [20, 30, 40]
print(numbers)  # Output: [1, 20, 30, 40, 5]
```

List Methods and Operations

Python provides several built-in methods and operations that you can use with lists. Here are some commonly used ones:

- `len(list)`: Returns the length (number of elements) of the list.
- `list.count(element)`: Returns the number of occurrences of the specified element in the list.

- `list.index(element)`: Returns the index of the first occurrence of the specified element in the list.
- `list.sort()`: Sorts the elements of the list in ascending order (modifies the original list).
- `list.reverse()`: Reverses the order of the elements in the list (modifies the original list).
- `sorted(list)`: Returns a new sorted list (does not modify the original list).
- `list.copy()`: Returns a shallow copy of the list.
- `list1 + list2`: Concatenates two lists and returns a new list.
- `element in list`: Checks if an element is present in the list (returns `True` or `False`).

```python
numbers = [3, 1, 4, 1, 5, 9, 2]

# Length of the list
print(len(numbers))   # Output: 7

# Count occurrences of 1
print(numbers.count(1))   # Output: 2

# Index of the first occurrence of 4
print(numbers.index(4))   # Output: 2

# Sort the list in ascending order
numbers.sort()
print(numbers)   # Output: [1, 1, 2, 3, 4, 5, 9]

# Reverse the order of elements
numbers.reverse()
print(numbers)   # Output: [9, 5, 4, 3, 2, 1, 1]

# Create a new sorted list
sorted_numbers = sorted(numbers)
print(sorted_numbers)   # Output: [1, 1, 2, 3, 4, 5, 9]

# Create a shallow copy
copy_numbers = numbers.copy()
print(copy_numbers)   # Output: [9, 5, 4, 3, 2, 1, 1]

# Concatenate two lists
combined_list = [10, 20] + numbers
print(combined_list)   # Output: [10, 20, 9, 5, 4, 3, 2, 1, 1]

# Check if an element is present
print(5 in numbers)   # Output: True
print(10 in numbers)   # Output: False
```

List Comprehensions

List comprehensions provide a concise way to create new lists by applying an expression to each element of an iterable (e.g., a list, tuple, or string). They can often replace the need for loops and make your code more readable and Pythonic.

The basic syntax for a list comprehension is:

```python
new_list = [expression for item in iterable]
```

Here's an example of creating a new list by squaring each element in an existing list:

```python
numbers = [1, 2, 3, 4, 5]
squared_numbers = [x  2 for x in numbers]
print(squared_numbers)  # Output: [1, 4, 9, 16, 25]
```

You can also include a condition in the list comprehension to filter elements:

```python
numbers = [1, 2, 3, 4, 5, 6, 7, 8, 9, 10]
even_numbers = [x for x in numbers if x % 2 == 0]
print(even_numbers)  # Output: [2, 4, 6, 8, 10]
```

List comprehensions can be nested to create more complex expressions:

```python
matrix = [[1, 2, 3], [4, 5, 6], [7, 8, 9]]
flattened = [num for row in matrix for num in row]
print(flattened)  # Output: [1, 2, 3, 4, 5, 6, 7, 8, 9]
```

In this example, the nested list comprehension `[num for row in matrix for num in row]` flattens the nested list `matrix` into a single list `flattened`.

List comprehensions can make your code more concise and readable, especially when working with complex transformations or filtering operations on lists.

Lists in Python are incredibly versatile and powerful data structures. They provide a wide range of methods and operations to manipulate and work with ordered collections of items. Whether you're dealing with simple lists or complex nested structures, Python's list functionality allows you to efficiently organize and process your data.

In the next section, we'll explore another important data structure in Python: tuples.

3.2 Tuples

In Python, a tuple is an ordered, immutable collection of items. It is similar to a list, but with a key difference: tuples are immutable, meaning their elements cannot be modified after they are created. This immutability makes tuples useful for storing data that should not be changed, such as constants or read-only values.

Creating Tuples

Tuples are created by enclosing items (elements) within parentheses `()` and separating them by commas. Here are some examples of creating tuples in Python:

```python
# Empty tuple
empty_tuple = ()

# Tuple with a single element (note the trailing comma)
single_element_tuple = (1,)

# Tuple of integers
numbers = (1, 2, 3, 4, 5)

# Tuple of strings
names = ("Alice", "Bob", "Charlie")

# Tuple with mixed data types
mixed_tuple = (1, "apple", 3.14, True)
```

Note that if you create a tuple with a single element without a trailing comma, Python will interpret it as the value itself, not a tuple. For example, `single_value = (1)` is treated as an integer, not a tuple with a single element.

You can also create tuples without using parentheses by separating the elements with commas:

```python
point = 3, 4  # Equivalent to point = (3, 4)
```

This feature is known as tuple packing, and it can be useful for creating tuples on the fly.

Accessing Tuple Elements

Like lists, you can access individual elements in a tuple using indexing. Indexing in Python starts from 0, so the first element has an index of 0, the second element has an index of 1, and so on.

```python
fruits = ("apple", "banana", "cherry")
```

```python
# Access the first element
print(fruits[0])   # Output: apple

# Access the second element
print(fruits[1])   # Output: banana

# Access the last element
print(fruits[-1])   # Output: cherry
```

Negative indices can be used to access elements from the end of the tuple. The index `-1` refers to the last element, `-2` refers to the second-to-last element, and so on.

You can also use slicing to access a range of elements in a tuple. The syntax is `tuple_name[start:stop:step]`, where `start` is the index to start from (inclusive), `stop` is the index to stop at (exclusive), and `step` is the step size (optional, defaults to 1).

```python
numbers = (1, 2, 3, 4, 5, 6, 7, 8, 9, 10)

# Slice from index 2 to index 6 (exclusive)
print(numbers[2:6])   # Output: (3, 4, 5, 6)

# Slice from the beginning to index 4 (exclusive)
print(numbers[:4])   # Output: (1, 2, 3, 4)

# Slice from index 6 to the end
print(numbers[6:])   # Output: (7, 8, 9, 10)

# Slice with a step size of 2
print(numbers[1:8:2])   # Output: (2, 4, 6, 8)
```

Immutability of Tuples

The key difference between tuples and lists is that tuples are immutable, meaning their elements cannot be modified after they are created. Attempting to modify a tuple element will result in a `TypeError`.

```python
numbers = (1, 2, 3)

# Trying to modify a tuple element
numbers[0] = 10   # Raises a TypeError: 'tuple' object does not support item assignment
```

However, while individual elements cannot be modified, the entire tuple can be reassigned to a new tuple:

```python
numbers = (1, 2, 3)
numbers = (4, 5, 6)   # Reassigning the tuple to a new tuple
print(numbers)   # Output: (4, 5, 6)
```

This reassignment creates a new tuple object and binds the variable `numbers` to the new object.

Tuple Unpacking

Python allows you to unpack the elements of a tuple into separate variables. This can be useful when you need to work with individual elements of a tuple.

```python
point = (3, 4)
x, y = point
print(x)   # Output: 3
print(y)   # Output: 4
```

In this example, the values `3` and `4` from the tuple `(3, 4)` are unpacked and assigned to the variables `x` and `y`, respectively.

You can also use tuple unpacking with other data structures, like lists, as long as the number of variables matches the number of elements:

```python
values = [1, 2, 3, 4, 5]
a, b, *rest = values
print(a)     # Output: 1
print(b)     # Output: 2
print(rest) # Output: [3, 4, 5]
```

In this case, the first two elements (`1` and `2`) are assigned to `a` and `b`, respectively, while the remaining elements are collected into a new list `rest`.

Tuple Methods and Operations

While tuples themselves are immutable, Python provides several built-in functions and operations that you can use with tuples:

- `len(tuple)`: Returns the length (number of elements) of the tuple.
- `tuple.count(element)`: Returns the number of occurrences of the specified element in the tuple.
- `tuple.index(element)`: Returns the index of the first occurrence of the specified element in the tuple.
- `tuple1 + tuple2`: Concatenates two tuples and returns a new tuple.
- `element in tuple`: Checks if an element is present in the tuple (returns `True` or `False`).
- `tuple(iterable)`: Creates a new tuple from an iterable (e.g., a list, string, or another tuple).

```python
numbers = (3, 1, 4, 1, 5, 9, 2)

# Length of the tuple
print(len(numbers))  # Output: 7

# Count occurrences of 1
print(numbers.count(1))  # Output: 2

# Index of the first occurrence of 4
print(numbers.index(4))  # Output: 2

# Concatenate two tuples
combined_tuple = (10, 20) + numbers
print(combined_tuple)  # Output: (10, 20, 3, 1, 4, 1, 5, 9, 2)

# Check if an element is present
print(5 in numbers)  # Output: True
print(10 in numbers)   # Output: False

# Create a tuple from a list
fruits = ["apple", "banana", "cherry"]
fruit_tuple = tuple(fruits)
print(fruit_tuple)  # Output: ('apple', 'banana', 'cherry')
```

Tuple Comprehensions

Similar to list comprehensions, Python also supports tuple comprehensions, which provide a concise way to create new tuples by applying an expression to each element of an iterable (e.g., a list, tuple, or string).

The basic syntax for a tuple comprehension is:

```python
new_tuple = (expression for item in iterable)
```

Here's an example of creating a new tuple by squaring each element in an existing tuple:

```python
numbers = (1, 2, 3, 4, 5)
squared_numbers = (x  2 for x in numbers)
print(tuple(squared_numbers))  # Output: (1, 4, 9, 16, 25)
```

Note that the result of a tuple comprehension is a generator expression, which is an iterator. To get the actual tuple, you need to convert it using the `tuple()` function.

You can also include a condition in the tuple comprehension to filter elements:

```python
numbers = (1, 2, 3, 4, 5, 6, 7, 8, 9, 10)
even_numbers = (x for x in numbers if x % 2 == 0)
print(tuple(even_numbers))  # Output: (2, 4, 6, 8, 10)
```

Tuple comprehensions can be nested to create more complex expressions:

```python
matrix = ((1, 2, 3), (4, 5, 6), (7, 8, 9))
flattened = (num for row in matrix for num in row)
print(tuple(flattened))  # Output: (1, 2, 3, 4, 5, 6, 7, 8, 9)
```

In this example, the nested tuple comprehension `(num for row in matrix for num in row)` flattens the nested tuple `matrix` into a single tuple.

Tuple comprehensions can make your code more concise and readable, especially when working with complex transformations or filtering operations on tuples.

When to Use Tuples

Tuples are useful in several situations:

1. Immutable Data: When you need to store data that should not be modified, tuples are a better choice than lists. Examples include constants, configuration settings, or read-only data structures.

2. Heterogeneous Data: Tuples can store elements of different data types, making them useful for representing heterogeneous data structures, such as records or database rows.

3. Hashable Objects: Tuples are hashable, meaning they can be used as keys in dictionaries or elements in sets. Lists, on the other hand, are not hashable because they are mutable.

4. Unpacking: Tuple unpacking makes it easy to work with multiple values simultaneously, especially when returning or passing multiple values from/to functions.

5. Performance: Tuples are slightly more efficient than lists in terms of memory usage and performance, especially when dealing with large datasets or when immutability is desirable.

6. Code Clarity: Using tuples can make your code more readable and self-documenting, as they clearly indicate that the data should not be modified.

However, tuples also have limitations. If you need to modify the elements of a collection, you should use a list instead. Additionally, tuples don't have as many built-in methods as lists, so you may need to convert them to lists or use other data structures for more complex operations.

3.3 Dictionaries

Dictionaries are one of the most versatile and powerful data structures in Python. They are unordered collections of key-value pairs, where each key is unique and associated with a corresponding value. Dictionaries are mutable, meaning you can add, remove, or modify their key-value pairs after creation. They are widely used in various applications, such as storing and retrieving data, representing real-world objects, and implementing caching mechanisms.

Creating Dictionaries

In Python, dictionaries are created by enclosing a comma-separated list of key-value pairs within curly braces `{}`. The key and value are separated by a colon `:`

```python
# Empty dictionary
empty_dict = {}

# Dictionary with integer keys
student_ids = {1: "Alice", 2: "Bob", 3: "Charlie"}

# Dictionary with string keys
phone_book = {"Alice": "123-4567", "Bob": "987-6543", "Charlie": "456-7890"}

# Dictionary with mixed keys
mixed_dict = {"name": "Alice", 1: [1, 2, 3], 2.0: True}
```

The keys in a dictionary must be immutable objects, such as strings, numbers, or tuples. The values, on the other hand, can be of any data type, including other dictionaries, lists, or custom objects.

Accessing Dictionary Values

To access the value associated with a key in a dictionary, you can use the square bracket notation `[]` along with the key.

```python
phone_book = {"Alice": "123-4567", "Bob": "987-6543", "Charlie": "456-7890"}

# Accessing a value by key
print(phone_book["Alice"])   # Output: 123-4567

# Attempting to access a non-existent key raises a KeyError
print(phone_book["Eve"])   # Raises KeyError: 'Eve'
```

To handle non-existent keys safely, you can use the `get()` method, which returns a default value (specified as the second argument) if the key is not found in the dictionary.

```python
```

```python
phone_book = {"Alice": "123-4567", "Bob": "987-6543", "Charlie": "456-7890"}

# Using get() to safely access a value
print(phone_book.get("Alice", "Not found"))  # Output: 123-4567
print(phone_book.get("Eve", "Not found"))    # Output: Not found
```

Modifying Dictionaries

Since dictionaries are mutable, you can add, modify, or remove key-value pairs after creating them.

Adding Key-Value Pairs

To add a new key-value pair to a dictionary, simply assign a value to a new key using the square bracket notation.

```python
phone_book = {"Alice": "123-4567", "Bob": "987-6543"}

# Adding a new key-value pair
phone_book["Charlie"] = "456-7890"
print(phone_book)  # Output: {'Alice': '123-4567', 'Bob': '987-6543',
'Charlie': '456-7890'}
```

Modifying Values

To modify the value associated with an existing key, assign a new value to that key using the square bracket notation.

```python
phone_book = {"Alice": "123-4567", "Bob": "987-6543", "Charlie": "456-7890"}

# Modifying the value of an existing key
phone_book["Bob"] = "111-2222"
print(phone_book)  # Output: {'Alice': '123-4567', 'Bob': '111-2222',
'Charlie': '456-7890'}
```

Removing Key-Value Pairs

To remove a key-value pair from a dictionary, you can use the `pop()` method or the `del` keyword.

The `pop()` method removes the key-value pair from the dictionary and returns the corresponding value. If the key is not found, it raises a `KeyError` unless a default value is provided as the second argument.

```python
phone_book = {"Alice": "123-4567", "Bob": "987-6543", "Charlie": "456-7890"}

# Removing a key-value pair using pop()
removed_value = phone_book.pop("Bob")
```

```python
print(removed_value)   # Output: 987-6543
print(phone_book)      # Output: {'Alice': '123-4567', 'Charlie': '456-7890'}
```

The `del` keyword removes the key-value pair from the dictionary without returning the value. If the key is not found, it raises a `KeyError`.

```python
phone_book = {"Alice": "123-4567", "Bob": "987-6543", "Charlie": "456-7890"}

# Removing a key-value pair using del
del phone_book["Bob"]
print(phone_book)   # Output: {'Alice': '123-4567', 'Charlie': '456-7890'}
```

Dictionary Methods and Operations

Python provides several built-in methods and operations that you can use with dictionaries.

Accessing Keys and Values

- `dict.keys()`: Returns a view object containing all the keys in the dictionary.
- `dict.values()`: Returns a view object containing all the values in the dictionary.
- `dict.items()`: Returns a view object containing all the key-value pairs in the dictionary as tuples.

```python
phone_book = {"Alice": "123-4567", "Bob": "987-6543", "Charlie": "456-7890"}

# Accessing keys
print(phone_book.keys())   # Output: dict_keys(['Alice', 'Bob', 'Charlie'])

# Accessing values
print(phone_book.values())   # Output: dict_values(['123-4567', '987-6543',
'456-7890'])

# Accessing key-value pairs
print(phone_book.items())   # Output: dict_items([('Alice', '123-4567'),
('Bob', '987-6543'), ('Charlie', '456-7890')])
```

Checking Key Existence

- `key in dict`: Returns `True` if the key is present in the dictionary, `False` otherwise.

```python
phone_book = {"Alice": "123-4567", "Bob": "987-6543", "Charlie": "456-7890"}

# Checking if a key exists
print("Alice" in phone_book)   # Output: True
print("Eve" in phone_book)     # Output: False
```

```
```

Other Dictionary Methods
- `dict.update(other_dict)`: Updates the dictionary with the key-value pairs from another dictionary.
- `dict.clear()`: Removes all key-value pairs from the dictionary.
- `dict.copy()`: Returns a shallow copy of the dictionary.

```python
phone_book = {"Alice": "123-4567", "Bob": "987-6543"}
new_entries = {"Charlie": "456-7890", "Eve": "555-1234"}

# Updating a dictionary with another dictionary
phone_book.update(new_entries)
print(phone_book)  # Output: {'Alice': '123-4567', 'Bob': '987-6543',
'Charlie': '456-7890', 'Eve': '555-1234'}

# Clearing a dictionary
phone_book.clear()
print(phone_book)  # Output: {}

# Creating a copy of a dictionary
original = {"a": 1, "b": 2}
copy_dict = original.copy()
print(copy_dict)  # Output: {'a': 1, 'b': 2}
```

Dictionary Comprehensions
Similar to list and tuple comprehensions, Python also supports dictionary comprehensions, which provide a concise way to create new dictionaries by applying an expression to each element of an iterable.

The basic syntax for a dictionary comprehension is:

```python
new_dict = {key_expression: value_expression for item in iterable}
```

Here's an example of creating a new dictionary by squaring the values of an existing dictionary:

```python
original_dict = {"a": 1, "b": 2, "c": 3}
squared_dict = {key: value  2 for key, value in original_dict.items()}
print(squared_dict)  # Output: {'a': 1, 'b': 4, 'c': 9}
```

You can also include a condition in the dictionary comprehension to filter elements:

```python
numbers = [1, 2, 3, 4, 5, 6, 7, 8, 9, 10]
```

```
even_dict = {num: num  2 for num in numbers if num % 2 == 0}
print(even_dict)  # Output: {2: 4, 4: 16, 6: 36, 8: 64, 10: 100}
```

Dictionary comprehensions can make your code more concise and readable, especially when working with complex transformations or filtering operations on dictionaries.

When to Use Dictionaries

Dictionaries are useful in various situations, including:

Representing Key-Value Pairs

Dictionaries are ideal for representing and storing key-value pairs, such as configuration settings, database records, or data mappings.

Caching and Lookup Tables

Dictionaries provide efficient key-based lookups, making them well-suited for implementing caching mechanisms or lookup tables.

Counting and Grouping

Dictionaries can be used to count the occurrences of elements in a collection or group data based on specific criteria.

Representing Objects

Dictionaries can be used to represent real-world objects and their properties, providing a flexible way to store and access related data.

Sparse Data Structures

Dictionaries can be used to represent sparse data structures, where only a subset of possible keys has associated values.

Associative Arrays

In some programming languages, dictionaries are referred to as "associative arrays" or "maps," as they provide a way to associate keys with values.

Replacing Switch Statements

In languages that support switch statements, dictionaries can be used as a more flexible and extensible alternative for mapping keys to values or actions.

While dictionaries are powerful and versatile, they have some limitations:

- Keys must be unique and immutable (e.g., strings, numbers, tuples).
- Dictionaries are unordered, so the order of key-value pairs is not guaranteed.
- Lookups by value are inefficient since dictionaries are designed for key-based lookups.

When you need to maintain order or perform efficient value-based lookups, other data structures like lists or sets may be more appropriate.

3.4 Sets

In Python, a set is an unordered collection of unique elements. Sets are similar to lists, but with two key differences: they do not allow duplicate elements, and their elements are unordered, meaning they do not have a specific order or index associated with them. Sets are mutable, meaning you can add or remove elements after creating the set, but you cannot modify individual elements directly. Sets are widely used in various applications, such as removing duplicates from a collection, performing mathematical operations (like unions, intersections, and differences) on collections, and implementing efficient membership testing.

Creating Sets

In Python, sets are created by enclosing a comma-separated list of elements within curly braces `{}` or by using the `set()` function.

```python
# Creating an empty set
empty_set = set()

# Creating a set with elements
fruits = {"apple", "banana", "cherry"}

# Creating a set from a list
numbers = set([1, 2, 3, 2, 4, 1])  # Output: {1, 2, 3, 4}

# Creating a set from a string (each character is an element)
characters = set("hello")  # Output: {'e', 'h', 'l', 'o'}
```

Note that if you create an empty set using curly braces without any elements (`{}`) Python interprets it as an empty dictionary. Therefore, it is recommended to use the `set()` function to create an empty set.

Adding Elements to a Set

To add a single element to a set, you can use the `add()` method.

```python
fruits = {"apple", "banana", "cherry"}

# Adding an element to the set
fruits.add("orange")
print(fruits)  # Output: {'banana', 'apple', 'cherry', 'orange'}
```

To add multiple elements to a set, you can use the `update()` method, which accepts an iterable (such as a list, tuple, or another set) as an argument.

```python
fruits = {"apple", "banana", "cherry"}

# Adding multiple elements to the set
more_fruits = ["mango", "kiwi", "banana"]  # Note: Duplicates are ignored
fruits.update(more_fruits)
print(fruits)  # Output: {'kiwi', 'cherry', 'apple', 'mango', 'banana'}
```

Removing Elements from a Set

To remove an element from a set, you can use the `remove()` or `discard()` methods.

The `remove()` method removes the specified element from the set. If the element is not present, it raises a `KeyError`.

```python
fruits = {"apple", "banana", "cherry"}

# Removing an element from the set using remove()
fruits.remove("banana")
print(fruits)  # Output: {'apple', 'cherry'}

# Trying to remove a non-existent element raises a KeyError
fruits.remove("grape")  # Raises KeyError: 'grape'
```

The `discard()` method also removes the specified element from the set, but it does not raise an error if the element is not present.

```python
fruits = {"apple", "banana", "cherry"}

# Removing an element from the set using discard()
fruits.discard("banana")
print(fruits)  # Output: {'apple', 'cherry'}

# Discarding a non-existent element does not raise an error
fruits.discard("grape")
print(fruits)  # Output: {'apple', 'cherry'}
```

You can also remove and return an arbitrary element from the set using the `pop()` method. This method is useful when you need to remove an element without knowing its value.

```python
fruits = {"apple", "banana", "cherry"}
```

```python
# Removing and returning an arbitrary element from the set
removed_fruit = fruits.pop()
print(removed_fruit)  # Output: 'apple' (or any other element from the set)
print(fruits)  # Output: {'banana', 'cherry'}
```

If you want to remove all elements from a set, you can use the `clear()` method.

```python
fruits = {"apple", "banana", "cherry"}

# Removing all elements from the set
fruits.clear()
print(fruits)  # Output: set()
```

Set Operations

Python supports various set operations that allow you to perform mathematical operations on sets. These operations are useful for tasks like finding common elements, removing duplicates, or combining collections.

Union

The union operation combines all unique elements from two or more sets. It can be performed using the `|` operator or the `union()` method.

```python
set1 = {1, 2, 3}
set2 = {3, 4, 5}

# Union using the | operator
union_set = set1 | set2
print(union_set)  # Output: {1, 2, 3, 4, 5}

# Union using the union() method
union_set = set1.union(set2)
print(union_set)  # Output: {1, 2, 3, 4, 5}
```

Intersection

The intersection operation returns a new set containing the common elements between two or more sets. It can be performed using the `&` operator or the `intersection()` method.

```python
set1 = {1, 2, 3}
set2 = {2, 3, 4}

# Intersection using the & operator
```

```python
intersection_set = set1 & set2
print(intersection_set)  # Output: {2, 3}

# Intersection using the intersection() method
intersection_set = set1.intersection(set2)
print(intersection_set)  # Output: {2, 3}
```

Difference

The difference operation returns a new set containing the elements that are present in one set but not in another. It can be performed using the `-` operator or the `difference()` method.

```python
set1 = {1, 2, 3}
set2 = {2, 3, 4}

# Difference using the - operator
difference_set = set1 - set2
print(difference_set)  # Output: {1}

# Difference using the difference() method
difference_set = set1.difference(set2)
print(difference_set)  # Output: {1}
```

Symmetric Difference

The symmetric difference operation returns a new set containing the elements that are present in either of the two sets, but not in both. It can be performed using the `^` operator or the `symmetric_difference()` method.

```python
set1 = {1, 2, 3}
set2 = {2, 3, 4}

# Symmetric difference using the ^ operator
symmetric_diff_set = set1 ^ set2
print(symmetric_diff_set)  # Output: {1, 4}

# Symmetric difference using the symmetric_difference() method
symmetric_diff_set = set1.symmetric_difference(set2)
print(symmetric_diff_set)  # Output: {1, 4}
```

Subset and Superset

The subset and superset operations allow you to check if one set is a subset or superset of another set, respectively.

The `issubset()` method returns `True` if all elements of a set are contained in another set.

```python
set1 = {1, 2, 3}
set2 = {1, 2, 3, 4, 5}

# Checking if set1 is a subset of set2
print(set1.issubset(set2))   # Output: True

# Checking if set2 is a subset of set1
print(set2.issubset(set1))   # Output: False
```

The `issuperset()` method returns `True` if a set contains all elements of another set.

```python
set1 = {1, 2, 3}
set2 = {1, 2, 3, 4, 5}

# Checking if set2 is a superset of set1
print(set2.issuperset(set1))   # Output: True

# Checking if set1 is a superset of set2
print(set1.issuperset(set2))   # Output: False
```

You can also use the `<=` operator to check if a set is a subset of another set, and the `>=` operator to check if a set is a superset of another set.

```python
set1 = {1, 2, 3}
set2 = {1, 2, 3, 4, 5}

# Checking if set1 is a subset of set2
print(set1 <= set2)   # Output: True

# Checking if set2 is a superset of set1
print(set2 >= set1)   # Output: True
```

Set Comprehensions

Similar to list and dictionary comprehensions, Python also supports set comprehensions, which provide a concise way to create new sets by applying an expression to each element of an iterable.

The basic syntax for a set comprehension is:

```python
new_set = {expression for item in iterable}
```

Here's an example of creating a new set by squaring each element in an existing set:

```python
original_set = {1, 2, 3}
squared_set = {x  2 for x in original_set}
print(squared_set)  # Output: {1, 4, 9}
```

You can also include a condition in the set comprehension to filter elements:

```python
numbers = [1, 2, 3, 4, 5, 6, 7, 8, 9, 10]
even_set = {num for num in numbers if num % 2 == 0}
print(even_set)  # Output: {2, 4, 6, 8, 10}
```

Set comprehensions can make your code more concise and readable, especially when working with complex transformations or filtering operations on sets.

When to Use Sets

Sets are useful in various situations, including:

Removing Duplicates

One of the most common use cases for sets is removing duplicate elements from a collection. Since sets only store unique elements, you can convert a list or other iterable to a set to remove duplicates.

```python
numbers = [1, 2, 3, 2, 4, 1, 5]
unique_numbers = set(numbers)
print(unique_numbers)  # Output: {1, 2, 3, 4, 5}
```

Membership Testing

Sets provide efficient membership testing, which means checking if an element is present in the set or not. This is particularly useful when working with large collections, as membership testing in sets is generally faster than in lists.

```python
fruits = {"apple", "banana", "cherry"}
print("apple" in fruits)  # Output: True
print("grape" in fruits)  # Output: False
```

Mathematical Operations

Sets support various mathematical operations, such as unions, intersections, differences, and symmetric differences. These operations are useful for tasks like finding common elements between collections, removing elements that exist in one collection but not in another, or combining collections while eliminating duplicates.

Counting Unique Elements

Sets can be used to count the number of unique elements in a collection by converting the collection to a set and checking its length.

```python
data = [1, 2, 3, 2, 4, 1, 5, 5, 5]
unique_count = len(set(data))
print(unique_count)  # Output: 5
```

Implementing Lookup Tables

Sets can be used to implement efficient lookup tables, where you can quickly check if an element exists in the set or not. This is particularly useful in scenarios where you need to perform frequent membership tests on a large collection of data.

While sets are powerful and versatile, they have some limitations:

- Sets are unordered, so you cannot access elements by index or maintain a specific order.
- Sets only store unique elements, so they are not suitable for scenarios where duplicates are allowed or required.
- Set operations involving large sets can be memory-intensive, as sets store all elements in memory.

When you need to maintain order or allow duplicates, other data structures like lists or tuples may be more appropriate. Additionally, if you need to store and retrieve key-value pairs, dictionaries are a better choice.

Exercise: Palindrome Checker

Write a function that takes a string as input and returns True if the string is a palindrome (reads the same forward and backward), and False otherwise. The function should be case-insensitive and ignore non-alphanumeric characters.

Solution:

```python
def is_palindrome(string):
    # Convert the string to lowercase and remove non-alphanumeric characters
    cleaned_string = ''.join(char for char in string.lower() if
char.isalnum())

    # Check if the cleaned string is equal to its reverse
    return cleaned_string == cleaned_string[::-1]

# Test cases
print(is_palindrome("A man a plan a canal Panama"))  # True
print(is_palindrome("Hello, World!"))  # False
```

```
print(is_palindrome("Race car"))   # True
print(is_palindrome("Step on no pets"))   # True
```

Explanation:

1. The is_palindrome function takes a string as input.
2. It converts the string to lowercase using the lower() method.
3. It removes non-alphanumeric characters (e.g., spaces, punctuation) from the string using a list comprehension and the isalnum() method.
4. The cleaned string is then compared with its reverse (obtained using the [::-1] slicing notation).
5. The function returns True if the cleaned string is equal to its reverse (meaning it's a palindrome), and False otherwise.
6. The provided test cases demonstrate the behavior of the function for different input strings.

Project: Word Count

Create a program that takes a text file as input and counts the occurrences of each word in the file. The program should output a dictionary or a list of tuples, where the keys are the words, and the values are the corresponding word counts.

Solution:

```
def count_words(file_path):
    word_counts = {}

    with open(file_path, 'r') as file:
        for line in file:
            words = line.strip().split()
            for word in words:
                word_counts[word.lower()] = word_counts.get(word.lower(), 0)
+ 1

    return word_counts


# Example usage
file_path = 'example.txt'
word_counts = count_words(file_path)

for word, count in word_counts.items():
    print(f"{word}: {count}")
```

Explanation:

1. The count_words function takes a file path as input.
2. It initializes an empty dictionary word_counts to store the word counts.
3. The function opens the file in read mode using the with statement and a for loop to iterate over each line in the file.
4. For each line, it splits the line into individual words using the split() method and the whitespace character as the delimiter.

5. For each word in the line, it updates the word_counts dictionary by converting the word to lowercase and incrementing its count.
6. The get method is used to retrieve the existing count for a word, or 0 if the word is not present in the dictionary.
7. After processing all lines, the function returns the word_counts dictionary.
8. In the example usage, the count_words function is called with a file path, and the resulting word_counts dictionary is printed.

Note: Make sure to have a text file named example.txt in the same directory as your Python script for this example to work correctly.

Chapter 4: Functions and Modules

In programming, functions are reusable blocks of code that perform specific tasks. They are essential for writing modular and maintainable code. Functions help you organize your code, avoid repetition, and make it easier to understand and debug. Python provides built-in functions and allows you to define your own custom functions.

4.1 Defining and Calling Functions

To define a function in Python, you use the `def` keyword followed by the function name, parentheses `()`, and a colon `:`. The code block that follows the colon is the function body, which contains the statements that will be executed when the function is called.

Here's the basic syntax for defining a function:

```python
def function_name(parameters):
    """Docstring explaining the function"""
    # Function body
    # Statements
    return value
```

- `def` is the keyword used to define a function.
- `function_name` is the name you give to the function, following Python's naming conventions (e.g., `calculate_area`).
- `parameters` (optional) are the input values that the function can accept, separated by commas and enclosed in parentheses. If the function doesn't require any parameters, the parentheses are left empty.
- `"""Docstring"""` (optional but recommended) is a string that provides a brief description of what the function does. It's a good practice to include docstrings to improve code readability and maintainability.
- The function body contains the statements that define the behavior of the function.
- `return` (optional) is used to specify the value that the function should return when it completes its execution. If no `return` statement is provided, the function implicitly returns `None`.

To call or invoke a function, you simply use its name followed by parentheses `()`. If the function requires arguments, you provide them inside the parentheses, separated by commas.

Here's an example of a simple function that calculates the area of a rectangle:

```python
def calculate_area(length, width):
    """Calculate the area of a rectangle."""
    area = length * width
    return area
```

```python
# Calling the function
rectangle_area = calculate_area(5, 3)
print(f"The area of the rectangle is: {rectangle_area}")  # Output: The area
of the rectangle is: 15
```

In this example, the `calculate_area` function takes two parameters: `length` and `width`. Inside the function body, it calculates the area by multiplying the `length` and `width` values, and then returns the result using the `return` statement. When the function is called with arguments `5` and `3`, it calculates the area (`5 * 3 = 15`) and assigns the result to the `rectangle_area` variable, which is then printed to the console.

4.2 Function Arguments and Return Values

Python supports several types of function arguments, including positional arguments, keyword arguments, and default arguments. Understanding these argument types will help you write more flexible and readable functions.

Positional Arguments

Positional arguments are the simplest way to pass arguments to a function. The values are assigned to the corresponding parameters based on their position in the argument list.

```python
def greet(name, age):
    print(f"Hello, {name}! You are {age} years old.")

greet("Alice", 25)  # Output: Hello, Alice! You are 25 years old.
```

In this example, `"Alice"` is assigned to the `name` parameter, and `25` is assigned to the `age` parameter based on their positions in the argument list.

Keyword Arguments

Keyword arguments allow you to specify the parameter names when calling a function. This can improve code readability and make it easier to understand the purpose of each argument.

```python
def greet(name, age):
    print(f"Hello, {name}! You are {age} years old.")

greet(name="Alice", age=25)  # Output: Hello, Alice! You are 25 years old.
```

Using keyword arguments makes it clear which value corresponds to which parameter, especially when the function has many parameters or when the arguments have non-obvious meanings.

Default Arguments

Default arguments allow you to provide a default value for a parameter in case no value is provided when the function is called. This can make your functions more flexible and easier to use.

```python
def greet(name, age=None):
    if age:
        print(f"Hello, {name}! You are {age} years old.")
    else:
        print(f"Hello, {name}!")

greet("Alice", 25)  # Output: Hello, Alice! You are 25 years old.
greet("Bob")  # Output: Hello, Bob!
```

In this example, the `age` parameter has a default value of `None`. If an age is provided when calling the function, it will print the age along with the greeting. If no age is provided, the function will print only the greeting without the age.

Return Values

The `return` statement is used to specify the value that a function should return when it completes its execution. Functions can return any data type, including strings, numbers, lists, dictionaries, or custom objects.

Here's an example of a function that calculates the sum of two numbers:

```python
def add_numbers(a, b):
    """Add two numbers and return the result."""
    sum = a + b
    return sum

result = add_numbers(3, 5)
print(f"The sum is: {result}")  # Output: The sum is: 8
```

In this example, the `add_numbers` function takes two parameters `a` and `b`, calculates their sum, and returns the result using the `return` statement. The returned value is then assigned to the `result` variable, which is printed to the console.

If a function doesn't have a `return` statement, or if the `return` statement is executed without a value, the function will implicitly return `None`.

4.3 Built-in Modules

Python comes with a vast standard library that includes many built-in modules. Modules are collections of functions, classes, and variables that provide specific functionality. Using built-in modules can save you time and effort by leveraging pre-written code for common tasks.

Here are some examples of commonly used built-in modules in Python:

1. `math` module

The `math` module provides functions for performing mathematical operations, such as trigonometric functions, logarithmic functions, and more.

```python
import math

x = 3.14
print(math.floor(x))   # Output: 3 (rounds down to the nearest integer)
print(math.sqrt(25))   # Output: 5.0 (square root of 25)
```

2. `random` module

The `random` module allows you to generate random numbers and make random choices from sequences.

```python
import random

print(random.randint(1, 10))   # Output: A random integer between 1 and 10
my_list = [1, 2, 3, 4, 5]
print(random.choice(my_list))   # Output: A random element from the list
```

3. `os` module

The `os` module provides a way to interact with the operating system, such as creating, deleting, or renaming files and directories.

```python
import os

print(os.getcwd())   # Output: Current working directory
os.mkdir("new_folder")   # Create a new folder
os.rename("file.txt", "renamed_file.txt")   # Rename a file
```

```
```

4. `datetime` module

The `datetime` module provides classes for working with dates and times.

```python
import datetime

today = datetime.date.today()
print(today)  # Output: Current date (e.g., 2023-03-07)

now = datetime.datetime.now()
print(now)  # Output: Current date and time (e.g., 2023-03-07 14:30:00)
```

These are just a few examples of the many built-in modules available in Python. You can explore the Python Standard Library documentation to learn about other modules and their functionalities.

4.4 Creating and Importing Custom Modules

In addition to using built-in modules, you can create your own custom modules to organize and reuse code across multiple Python files. This promotes code modularity, maintainability, and code reuse.

Creating a Custom Module

To create a custom module in Python, you simply create a new Python file with the desired functionality. For example, let's create a module called `geometry.py` that contains functions for calculating the area and perimeter of different shapes.

```python
# geometry.py

def calculate_rectangle_area(length, width):
    """Calculate the area of a rectangle."""
    area = length * width
    return area

def calculate_rectangle_perimeter(length, width):
    """Calculate the perimeter of a rectangle."""
    perimeter = 2 * (length + width)
    return perimeter

def calculate_circle_area(radius):
    """Calculate the area of a circle."""
    import math
    area = math.pi * radius ** 2
```

```
    return area
```

Importing Custom Modules

To use the functions from your custom module in another Python file, you need to import the module. There are several ways to import a module:

1. Import the entire module

```python
import geometry

rectangle_area = geometry.calculate_rectangle_area(5, 3)
circle_area = geometry.calculate_circle_area(2)
```

2. Import specific functions from a module

```python
from geometry import calculate_rectangle_area, calculate_circle_area

rectangle_area = calculate_rectangle_area(5, 3)
circle_area = calculate_circle_area(2)
```

3. Import all functions from a module using wildcard `*` (not recommended)

```python
from geometry import *

rectangle_area = calculate_rectangle_area(5, 3)
circle_area = calculate_circle_area(2)
```

While the wildcard import (`from module import *`) is convenient, it can lead to naming conflicts and make it harder to understand where specific functions or variables come from. It's generally better to import modules or specific functions explicitly.

Module Paths

When importing a custom module, Python searches for the module in several locations, including the current directory and the directories listed in the `sys.path` list. If your module is in a different directory, you need to provide the full path or add the directory to the `sys.path` list.

For example, if your `geometry.py` module is in a folder called `mymodules`, you can import it like this:

```python
import sys
sys.path.append("path/to/mymodules")
import geometry

rectangle_area = geometry.calculate_rectangle_area(5, 3)
```

Alternatively, you can use the full path when importing the module:

```python
from mymodules.geometry import calculate_rectangle_area

rectangle_area = calculate_rectangle_area(5, 3)
```

Package Importing

Python also supports organizing modules into packages, which are directories containing an `__init__.py` file. Packages allow you to group related modules together and provide a hierarchical namespace for better organization and code reuse.

For example, you could have a package called `geometry` with separate modules for different shapes:

```
geometry/
    __init__.py
    rectangle.py
    circle.py
```

In the `__init__.py` file, you can import and re-export specific functions or modules from the package:

```python
# __init__.py
from .rectangle import calculate_rectangle_area,
calculate_rectangle_perimeter
from .circle import calculate_circle_area
```

Now, you can import functions directly from the `geometry` package:

```python
import geometry

rectangle_area = geometry.calculate_rectangle_area(5, 3)
circle_area = geometry.calculate_circle_area(2)
```

By creating custom modules and packages, you can organize your code, promote code reuse, and make it easier to maintain and share your Python projects.

Practical Examples

To solidify your understanding of functions and modules, let's explore some practical examples.

Example 1: Calculator Module

Imagine you want to create a simple calculator module that performs basic arithmetic operations. You can define functions for addition, subtraction, multiplication, and division, and then import and use these functions in your main program.

```python
# calculator.py (module)

def add(a, b):
    """Add two numbers."""
    return a + b

def subtract(a, b):
    """Subtract two numbers."""
    return a - b

def multiply(a, b):
    """Multiply two numbers."""
    return a * b

def divide(a, b):
    """Divide two numbers."""
    if b == 0:
        return "Cannot divide by zero!"
    return a / b
```

Now, you can import and use these functions in your main program:

```python
# main.py
import calculator

result = calculator.add(5, 3)
print(f"5 + 3 = {result}")  # Output: 5 + 3 = 8

result = calculator.subtract(10, 4)
print(f"10 - 4 = {result}")  # Output: 10 - 4 = 6
```

```python
result = calculator.multiply(2, 6)
print(f"2 * 6 = {result}")   # Output: 2 * 6 = 12

result = calculator.divide(15, 3)
print(f"15 / 3 = {result}")   # Output: 15 / 3 = 5.0

result = calculator.divide(10, 0)
print(result)   # Output: Cannot divide by zero!
```

Example 2: Student Management System

Let's consider a more complex example of a student management system. You can create separate modules for different functionalities, such as managing student records, calculating grades, and generating reports.

```python
# student.py (module)

class Student:
    def __init__(self, name, id, grades):
        self.name = name
        self.id = id
        self.grades = grades

    def calculate_average(self):
        """Calculate the average grade for the student."""
        total = sum(self.grades)
        average = total / len(self.grades)
        return average

# grades.py (module)

def calculate_class_average(students):
    """Calculate the average grade for a class of students."""
    total_grades = 0
    total_students = len(students)

    for student in students:
        total_grades += sum(student.grades)

    class_average = total_grades / (total_students * len(student.grades))
    return class_average

# report.py (module)

def generate_report(students):
```

```python
    """Generate a report for a class of students."""
    report = ""
    for student in students:
        report += f"Name: {student.name}, ID: {student.id}, Average Grade:
{student.calculate_average():.2f}\n"

    class_average = calculate_class_average(students)
    report += f"\nClass Average: {class_average:.2f}"

    return report

# main.py
from student import Student
from report import generate_report

# Create some students
student1 = Student("Alice", "123456", [85, 92, 78])
student2 = Student("Bob", "654321", [76, 88, 95])
student3 = Student("Charlie", "987654", [90, 82, 89])

students = [student1, student2, student3]

# Generate and print the report
report = generate_report(students)
print(report)
```

In this example, the `student.py` module defines the `Student` class with methods for calculating the average grade for a student. The `grades.py` module contains a function for calculating the average grade for a class of students. The `report.py` module provides a function for generating a report with individual student grades and the class average.

In the `main.py` file, you create instances of `Student` objects, store them in a list, and then use the `generate_report` function from the `report` module to generate and print a report for the class.

By organizing the code into separate modules, you can easily maintain and extend the functionality of the student management system. For example, you could add new modules for handling user input, saving data to a file, or generating different types of reports.

Exercise: Recursive Fibonacci Sequence

Write a function that takes a non-negative integer n as input and returns the nth number in the Fibonacci sequence using recursion. The Fibonacci sequence is a series of numbers in which each number is the sum of the two preceding ones, usually starting with 0 and 1.

Solution:

```python
def fibonacci(n):
```

```python
    if n <= 0:
        return 0
    elif n == 1:
        return 1
    else:
        return fibonacci(n - 1) + fibonacci(n - 2)

# Test cases
print(fibonacci(0))    # 0
print(fibonacci(1))    # 1
print(fibonacci(5))    # 5
print(fibonacci(10))   # 55
```

Explanation:

1. The fibonacci function takes a non-negative integer n as input.
2. The function uses recursion to calculate the nth Fibonacci number.
3. The base cases are:
    - If n is 0 or less, the function returns 0.
    - If n is 1, the function returns 1.
4. For all other cases, the function recursively calls itself with n - 1 and n - 2 and returns the sum of the results.
5. The provided test cases demonstrate the behavior of the function for different input values.

Project: Module for Arithmetic Operations

Create a Python module named arithmetic_operations.py that defines functions for performing basic arithmetic operations (addition, subtraction, multiplication, and division). The module should also include a function to calculate the power of a number. Then, create another Python script that imports and uses the functions from the arithmetic_operations module.

Solution:

```python
arithmetic_operations.py:
python
Copy code
def add(a, b):
    return a + b

def subtract(a, b):
    return a - b

def multiply(a, b):
    return a * b

def divide(a, b):
    if b != 0:
        return a / b
    else:
```

```python
        raise ZeroDivisionError("Cannot divide by zero")

def power(base, exponent):
    return base ** exponent
```

main.py:

```python
import arithmetic_operations as ao

num1 = float(input("Enter the first number: "))
num2 = float(input("Enter the second number: "))

print(f"{num1} + {num2} = {ao.add(num1, num2)}")
print(f"{num1} - {num2} = {ao.subtract(num1, num2)}")
print(f"{num1} * {num2} = {ao.multiply(num1, num2)}")

try:
    print(f"{num1} / {num2} = {ao.divide(num1, num2)}")
except ZeroDivisionError as e:
    print(e)

base = float(input("Enter the base: "))
exponent = float(input("Enter the exponent: "))

print(f"{base} ^ {exponent} = {ao.power(base, exponent)}")
```

Explanation:

1. The arithmetic_operations.py file defines five functions:
   - add(a, b): Returns the sum of a and b.
   - subtract(a, b): Returns the difference between a and b.
   - multiply(a, b): Returns the product of a and b.
   - divide(a, b): Returns the quotient of a divided by b. If b is zero, it raises a ZeroDivisionError.
   - power(base, exponent): Returns the result of raising base to the power of exponent.
2. The main.py file imports the arithmetic_operations module and assigns it an alias ao.
3. The script prompts the user to enter two numbers and performs arithmetic operations (addition, subtraction, multiplication, and division) using the functions from the arithmetic_operations module.
4. If division by zero occurs, the divide function raises a ZeroDivisionError, which is caught and handled in the try-except block.
5. The script then prompts the user to enter a base and an exponent and calculates the power using the power function from the arithmetic_operations module.

Chapter 5: File Handling

5.1 Reading from Files

In the realm of computer programming, file handling is a fundamental concept that allows developers to interact with data stored on a computer's file system. One of the most common operations in file handling is reading from files, which involves retrieving data stored in a file and making it available for processing or analysis within a program. This article aims to provide a comprehensive guide for absolute beginners on reading from files, covering essential concepts, techniques, and best practices.

Understanding Files and File Systems

Before delving into the intricacies of reading from files, it's crucial to understand what files are and how they are organized within a file system. A file is a collection of data stored on a computer's storage medium, such as a hard disk drive (HDD), solid-state drive (SSD), or cloud storage. Files can contain various types of data, including text documents, images, audio, video, and more.

The file system is a hierarchical structure that organizes files and directories (also known as folders) on a storage medium. It provides a logical way to store, retrieve, and manage files. Files are typically organized into directories, which can contain subdirectories and files. Each file and directory has a unique name and path that identifies its location within the file system.

Opening Files for Reading

To read data from a file, you first need to open the file in a specific mode. In most programming languages, there are built-in functions or methods that allow you to open files. In Python, for example, you can use the `open()` function to open a file for reading. Here's an example:

```python
file = open("example.txt", "r")
```

In this example, `open("example.txt", "r")` opens a file named `example.txt` in read mode, denoted by the `"r"` parameter. The `open()` function returns a file object that represents the opened file.

It's important to note that when you open a file, the file must exist in the specified location. If the file does not exist or the path is incorrect, you may encounter an error.

Reading File Contents

Once you have opened a file for reading, you can read its contents using various methods or functions provided by the programming language. Here are some common techniques for reading file contents:

1. Reading the entire file at once:

This approach reads the entire contents of the file into memory as a single string or list of lines. While convenient for small files, it may not be suitable for large files due to memory limitations.

In Python, you can use the `read()` method to read the entire file contents as a string:

```python
file = open("example.txt", "r")
content = file.read()
print(content)
file.close()
```

Alternatively, you can use the `readlines()` method to read the file contents as a list of lines:

```python
file = open("example.txt", "r")
lines = file.readlines()
for line in lines:
    print(line)
file.close()
```

2. Reading files line by line:

This approach reads the file contents one line at a time, which is useful for processing large files or when you don't need to load the entire file into memory at once.

In Python, you can use a `for` loop to iterate over the file object line by line:

```python
file = open("example.txt", "r")
for line in file:
    print(line)
file.close()
```

3. Reading a specific number of characters or bytes:

Some programming languages allow you to read a specific number of characters or bytes from a file at a time. This can be useful when working with binary data or when you need to process data in smaller chunks.

In Python, you can use the `read(n)` method to read `n` bytes from the file:

```python
file = open("example.txt", "r")
chunk = file.read(10)  # Read the first 10 bytes
print(chunk)
file.close()
```

Closing Files

After you have finished reading from a file, it's important to close the file properly. Closing a file ensures that any resources associated with the file, such as memory buffers or file handles, are released and made available for other operations. Failing to close files can lead to resource leaks and other issues.

In most programming languages, you can close a file using a dedicated function or method. In Python, you can use the `close()` method:

```python
file = open("example.txt", "r")
content = file.read()
print(content)
file.close()
```

It's considered a best practice to use the `with` statement when working with files in Python. This statement automatically takes care of closing the file when the code block is exited, even in the case of exceptions or errors:

```python
with open("example.txt", "r") as file:
    content = file.read()
    print(content)
```

By using the `with` statement, you don't need to explicitly call the `close()` method, as it is handled automatically by the context manager.

File Encoding and Character Encodings

When reading text files, it's important to consider character encodings. Character encoding is a way of representing text data as a sequence of bytes or binary code. Different encoding schemes, such as ASCII, UTF-8, and UTF-16, define different ways of mapping characters to binary representations.

If you're working with text files that contain non-ASCII characters, such as accented characters or non-Latin scripts, you need to ensure that the character encoding is correctly specified when opening the file. Otherwise, you may encounter encoding errors or incorrect character rendering.

In Python, you can specify the encoding when opening a file using the `encoding` parameter:

```python
with open("example.txt", "r", encoding="utf-8") as file:
    content = file.read()
    print(content)
```

In this example, the file is opened with the `"utf-8"` encoding, which is a commonly used Unicode encoding that supports a wide range of characters.

Handling Errors and Exceptions

When working with files, it's essential to handle errors and exceptions that may occur during the reading process. These errors can arise due to various reasons, such as file not found, permission issues, or read errors.

In most programming languages, you can use exception handling mechanisms to catch and handle exceptions gracefully. In Python, you can use the `try`/`except` statement to catch and handle exceptions:

```python
try:
    with open("example.txt", "r") as file:
        content = file.read()
        print(content)
except FileNotFoundError:
    print("Error: File not found.")
except IOError:
    print("Error: Unable to read the file.")
```

In this example, the code attempts to open the file `"example.txt"` and read its contents. If the file is not found, a `FileNotFoundError` exception is caught and handled. If there is an input/output error during the reading process, an `IOError` exception is caught and handled.

By handling exceptions properly, you can provide more robust and user-friendly error handling in your programs, making it easier to identify and troubleshoot issues related to file reading operations.

Best Practices for Reading Files

While reading from files is a fundamental operation, there are several best practices to follow to ensure efficient, secure, and maintainable code:

1. Use context managers or try/finally blocks: Always use context managers (e.g., `with` statement in Python) or `try`/`finally` blocks to ensure that files are properly closed after reading, even in the case of exceptions or errors.

2. Validate file paths and permissions: Before attempting to read a file, ensure that the file path is valid and that you have the necessary permissions to access the file.

3. Handle character encodings: When reading text files, be aware of character encodings and specify the correct encoding when opening the file to avoid encoding-related issues.

4. Use appropriate file reading techniques: Choose the appropriate file reading technique based on the size of the file and the requirements of your program. Reading the entire file at once may not be suitable for large files, while reading line by line or in smaller chunks can be more memory-efficient.

5. Implement error handling and logging: Properly handle exceptions and errors that may occur during file reading operations. Log relevant information to aid in debugging and troubleshooting.

6. Consider performance implications: Be mindful of performance implications when reading large files or when reading files frequently. Optimize your code by using appropriate buffering techniques or by reading files in smaller chunks when necessary.

7. Maintain code organization and readability: Organize your file reading code in a clear and readable manner, using consistent naming conventions, comments, and modular design principles.

8. Secure file operations: When working with sensitive data or files, implement appropriate security measures, such as validating user input, sanitizing file paths, and restricting access to sensitive files or directories.

9. Test your code thoroughly: Thoroughly test your file reading code with various scenarios, including edge cases, error conditions, and different file types and sizes, to ensure its robustness and correctness.

5.2 Writing to Files

In the realm of computer programming, file handling is a fundamental skill that enables developers to interact with data stored on a computer's file system. While reading from files is a crucial aspect of file handling, writing to files is equally important, as it allows programmers to create, modify, and update data stored in files. This article aims to provide a comprehensive guide for absolute beginners on writing to files, covering essential concepts, techniques, and best practices.

Understanding File Writing

Writing to a file involves creating a new file or modifying the contents of an existing file by appending, overwriting, or inserting data. This process is essential for various applications, such as logging system events, storing user data, generating reports, or creating backups.

To write to a file, you typically follow these steps:

1. Open the file in the appropriate mode (e.g., write, append, or create/overwrite).
2. Write data to the file using the provided functions or methods in your programming language.
3. Close the file after writing is complete.

Opening Files for Writing

Before writing to a file, you need to open the file in the appropriate mode. In most programming languages, there are built-in functions or methods that allow you to open files. In Python, for example, you can use the `open()` function to open a file for writing. Here are the common modes for opening files for writing:

1. Write mode (`"w"`): This mode opens a file for writing. If the file exists, its contents are truncated (deleted). If the file does not exist, a new file is created.

```python
```

```python
file = open("example.txt", "w")
```

2. Append mode (`"a"`): This mode opens a file for writing, but the new data is appended to the end of the existing file. If the file does not exist, a new file is created.

```python
file = open("example.txt", "a")
```

3. Create/overwrite mode (`"x"`): This mode creates a new file for writing. If the file already exists, an error is raised.

```python
file = open("example.txt", "x")
```

Writing File Contents

Once you have opened a file for writing, you can write data to the file using various methods or functions provided by the programming language. Here are some common techniques for writing to files:

1. Writing strings:

You can write strings to a file using the `write()` method in Python:

```python
file = open("example.txt", "w")
file.write("Hello, World!")
file.close()
```

2. Writing multiple strings:

To write multiple strings to a file, you can call the `write()` method multiple times or use a loop:

```python
file = open("example.txt", "w")
file.write("Line 1\n")
file.write("Line 2\n")
file.close()
```

3. Writing lists or other iterables:

If you have data in the form of lists or other iterables, you can use a loop to write each item to the file:

```python
data = ["Apple", "Banana", "Cherry"]
file = open("example.txt", "w")
for item in data:
```

```python
        file.write(item + "\n")
    file.close()
```

Closing Files

After you have finished writing to a file, it's crucial to close the file properly. Closing a file ensures that any data buffers are flushed, and the file is properly saved and closed, releasing any associated resources.

In most programming languages, you can close a file using a dedicated function or method. In Python, you can use the `close()` method:

```python
file = open("example.txt", "w")
file.write("Hello, World!")
file.close()
```

It's considered a best practice to use the `with` statement when working with files in Python. This statement automatically takes care of closing the file when the code block is exited, even in the case of exceptions or errors:

```python
with open("example.txt", "w") as file:
    file.write("Hello, World!")
```

By using the `with` statement, you don't need to explicitly call the `close()` method, as it is handled automatically by the context manager.

Handling Errors and Exceptions

When working with files, it's essential to handle errors and exceptions that may occur during the writing process. These errors can arise due to various reasons, such as file permission issues, disk full errors, or input/output errors.

In most programming languages, you can use exception handling mechanisms to catch and handle exceptions gracefully. In Python, you can use the `try`/`except` statement to catch and handle exceptions:

```python
try:
    with open("example.txt", "w") as file:
        file.write("Hello, World!")
except IOError:
    print("Error: Unable to write to the file.")
except Exception as e:
    print(f"An error occurred: {e}")
```

```
```

In this example, the code attempts to open the file `"example.txt"` in write mode and write the string `"Hello, World!"` to it. If there is an input/output error during the writing process, an `IOError` exception is caught and handled. If any other exception occurs, it is caught and handled by the general `Exception` block.

By handling exceptions properly, you can provide more robust and user-friendly error handling in your programs, making it easier to identify and troubleshoot issues related to file writing operations.

Best Practices for Writing to Files

While writing to files is a fundamental operation, there are several best practices to follow to ensure efficient, secure, and maintainable code:

1. **Use context managers or try/finally blocks:** Always use context managers (e.g., `with` statement in Python) or `try`/`finally` blocks to ensure that files are properly closed after writing, even in the case of exceptions or errors.

2. **Validate file paths and permissions:** Before attempting to write to a file, ensure that the file path is valid and that you have the necessary permissions to create or modify the file.

3. **Handle file existence and overwriting:** Be cautious when opening files in write mode, as it will overwrite the existing file contents. Consider using the appropriate mode (e.g., append mode or create/overwrite mode) based on your requirements.

4. **Implement error handling and logging:** Properly handle exceptions and errors that may occur during file writing operations. Log relevant information to aid in debugging and troubleshooting.

5. **Consider performance implications:** Be mindful of performance implications when writing large amounts of data to files or when writing to files frequently. Optimize your code by using appropriate buffering techniques or by writing data in batches when necessary.

6. **Maintain code organization and readability:** Organize your file writing code in a clear and readable manner, using consistent naming conventions, comments, and modular design principles.

7. **Secure file operations:** When working with sensitive data or files, implement appropriate security measures, such as validating user input, sanitizing file paths, and restricting access to sensitive files or directories.

8. **Test your code thoroughly:** Thoroughly test your file writing code with various scenarios, including edge cases, error conditions, and different file types and sizes, to ensure its robustness and correctness.

5.3 Python Working with CSV and JSON Files

In the world of data handling and processing, working with structured data formats is a crucial aspect of modern software development. Two widely used formats for storing and exchanging data are CSV (Comma-Separated Values) and JSON (JavaScript Object Notation). Python, being a versatile and powerful programming language, provides excellent support for working with these formats through its built-in modules and third-party libraries. This article aims to provide a comprehensive guide for absolute beginners on working with CSV and JSON files in Python, covering essential concepts, techniques, and best practices.

Understanding CSV Files

CSV is a simple and widely adopted file format for storing tabular data, such as spreadsheets or databases, in a plain-text format. CSV files represent data in a tabular form, with each row representing a record, and each column representing a field or attribute. The columns are separated by a delimiter, typically a comma (,), but other delimiters like semicolons (;) or tabs can also be used.

Python provides the built-in `csv` module for reading and writing CSV files. This module offers a convenient and efficient way to handle CSV data, abstracting away the low-level details of parsing and formatting CSV data.

1. Reading CSV Files:
To read data from a CSV file, you can use the `csv.reader()` function. Here's an example:

```python
import csv

with open('students.csv', 'r') as csvfile:
    csvreader = csv.reader(csvfile)
    for row in csvreader:
        print(row)
```

In this example, the `open()` function is used in conjunction with the `with` statement to open the `students.csv` file in read mode (`'r'`). The `csv.reader()` function is then used to create a reader object `csvreader`, which can iterate over the rows of the CSV file.

You can also handle different delimiters and other options by passing additional arguments to the `csv.reader()` function.

2. Writing CSV Files:
To write data to a CSV file, you can use the `csv.writer()` function. Here's an example:

```python
import csv

data = [['Name', 'Age', 'Grade'],
        ['Alice', 18, 'A'],
```

```
        ['Bob', 19, 'B'],
        ['Charlie', 17, 'A+']]

  with open('students.csv', 'w', newline='') as csvfile:
      csvwriter = csv.writer(csvfile)
      csvwriter.writerows(data)
  ```
```

In this example, a list of lists `data` is created, representing the data to be written to the CSV file. The `open()` function is used to create a new file named `students.csv` in write mode (`'w'`), and the `newline=''` argument is passed to avoid adding extra blank lines between rows.

The `csv.writer()` function is then used to create a writer object `csvwriter`, which can write rows to the CSV file using the `writerows()` method.

## Understanding JSON Files

JSON (JavaScript Object Notation) is a lightweight, human-readable data interchange format that is widely used for representing structured data. JSON is particularly popular for transmitting data between a server and web application or for storing configuration data in applications.

JSON data is represented as key-value pairs, where the values can be strings, numbers, booleans, objects (nested key-value pairs), or arrays (ordered collections of values). Here's an example of a JSON object representing a person's information:

```json
{
  "name": "Alice",
  "age": 30,
  "isStudent": true,
  "skills": ["Python", "JavaScript", "SQL"],
  "address": {
    "city": "New York",
    "country": "USA"
  }
}
```

In this example, the JSON object has various key-value pairs, including strings (`"name"`, `"city"`, `"country"`), numbers (`"age"`), booleans (`"isStudent"`), arrays (`"skills"`), and nested objects (`"address"`).

Python provides the built-in `json` module for working with JSON data. This module allows you to parse JSON data from strings or files, and convert Python objects into JSON representations.

1. Reading JSON Files:

To read data from a JSON file, you can use the `json.load()` function. Here's an example:
```

```python
import json

with open('person.json', 'r') as jsonfile:
    data = json.load(jsonfile)

print(data)
```

In this example, the `open()` function is used to open the `person.json` file in read mode (`'r'`). The `json.load()` function is then used to parse the JSON data from the file and store it in the `data` variable as a Python dictionary or list, depending on the structure of the JSON data.

2. Writing JSON Files:

To write data to a JSON file, you can use the `json.dump()` function. Here's an example:

```python
import json

person = {
    "name": "Alice",
    "age": 30,
    "isStudent": True,
    "skills": ["Python", "JavaScript", "SQL"],
    "address": {
        "city": "New York",
        "country": "USA"
    }
}

with open('person.json', 'w') as jsonfile:
    json.dump(person, jsonfile, indent=4)
```

In this example, a Python dictionary `person` is created, representing the data to be written to the JSON file. The `open()` function is used to create a new file named `person.json` in write mode (`'w'`).

The `json.dump()` function is then used to write the `person` dictionary to the JSON file. The `indent=4` argument is passed to make the output JSON more human-readable by adding indentation.

Advanced Features and Best Practices

While the built-in `csv` and `json` modules in Python provide basic functionality for working with CSV and JSON files, there are additional features and best practices that can enhance your experience and improve the robustness and maintainability of your code.

1. Handling Encoding:

When working with text data, it's essential to handle character encoding properly to avoid issues with non-ASCII characters. Both the `csv` and `json` modules provide options to specify the encoding when reading or writing files.

For CSV files, you can use the `encoding` parameter with `csv.reader()` or `csv.writer()`:

```python
with open('data.csv', 'r', encoding='utf-8') as csvfile:
    csvreader = csv.reader(csvfile)
    # ...
```

For JSON files, you can use the `encoding` parameter with `json.load()` or `json.dump()`:

```python
with open('data.json', 'r', encoding='utf-8') as jsonfile:
    data = json.load(jsonfile)
```

2. Handling Errors and Exceptions:

It's essential to handle errors and exceptions that may occur when reading or writing files. This can include file not found errors, permission issues, or invalid data formats. You can use Python's exception handling mechanisms, such as `try`/`except` blocks, to catch and handle exceptions gracefully.

3. Working with Large Files:

When working with large CSV or JSON files, it's recommended to use iterative or streaming approaches to avoid loading the entire file into memory at once. This can help prevent memory issues and improve performance.

For CSV files, you can use the `csv.reader()` function directly on the file object to read rows iteratively:

```python
with open('large_data.csv', 'r') as csvfile:
    csvreader = csv.reader(csvfile)
    for row in csvreader:
        # Process each row
        # ...
```

For JSON files, you can use the `json.load()` function with the `fp` argument to load data iteratively from a file-like object:

```python
with open('large_data.json', 'r') as jsonfile:
    data = json.load(jsonfile)
    for item in data:
        # Process each item
```

```
        # ...
```

4. Serializing Custom Python Objects:

The `json` module allows you to serialize and deserialize custom Python objects by defining custom encoder and decoder functions. This is particularly useful when working with complex data structures or custom classes.

5. Using Third-Party Libraries:

While the built-in `csv` and `json` modules are powerful and sufficient for most use cases, there are third-party libraries that provide additional features and enhanced functionality. For example, the `pandas` library offers extensive support for working with tabular data, including reading and writing CSV files, while the `simplejson` library provides additional features for working with JSON data.

6. Validating and Sanitizing Input Data:

When working with user-provided or external data, it's important to validate and sanitize the input data to prevent security vulnerabilities and ensure data integrity. This can include checking for malformed or malicious data, handling missing or unexpected values, and applying appropriate data validation techniques.

7. Documenting and Testing:

As with any code, it's essential to document your code and write unit tests to ensure the correctness and maintainability of your CSV and JSON handling functions. Clear documentation and comprehensive tests can help prevent bugs, facilitate collaboration, and make it easier to maintain and extend your codebase.

Exercise: Log File Analysis

Write a Python program that reads a log file and analyzes its contents. The program should:
1. Count the total number of log entries.
2. Count the number of log entries for each log level (e.g., INFO, WARNING, ERROR).
3. Find the most frequently occurring log message.

Solution:

```python
from collections import Counter

def analyze_log_file(file_path):
    log_entries = 0
    log_levels = Counter()
    log_messages = Counter()

    with open(file_path, 'r') as log_file:
        for line in log_file:
            log_entries += 1
            level, message = line.strip().split(': ', 1)
            log_levels[level] += 1
```

```
            log_messages[message] += 1

    print(f"Total log entries: {log_entries}")
    print("\nLog entries by level:")
    for level, count in log_levels.items():
        print(f"{level}: {count}")

    most_frequent_message = max(log_messages.items(), key=lambda x: x[1])
    print(f"\nMost frequent log message: \"{most_frequent_message[0]}\"
({most_frequent_message[1]} occurrences)")

# Example usage
analyze_log_file('example.log')
```

Explanation:

1. The analyze_log_file function takes the file path of the log file as input.
2. It initializes variables to store the total number of log entries (log_entries), a dictionary to count log entries by level (log_levels), and a dictionary to count log messages (log_messages).
3. The function opens the log file using the with statement and a for loop to iterate over each line in the file.
4. For each line, it increments the log_entries counter and splits the line into the log level and log message using the split method.
5. The log level and log message are then counted using the Counter objects log_levels and log_messages, respectively.
6. After processing all lines, the function prints the total number of log entries.
7. It then prints the number of log entries for each log level using a loop over the log_levels dictionary.
8. The most frequent log message is found by using the max function with a key function that returns the count of each message from the log_messages dictionary.
9. Finally, the most frequent log message and its count are printed.

Project: CSV File Processing

Write a Python program that reads data from a CSV file, performs some operations on the data, and writes the processed data to a new CSV file. The program should:

1. Read data from a CSV file containing student information (name, age, grade).
2. Calculate the average age and grade for all students.
3. Write a new CSV file with the original student data and two additional columns for the average age and average grade.

Solution:

```
import csv

def process_student_data(input_file, output_file):
    with open(input_file, 'r') as csv_file:
        reader = csv.reader(csv_file)
```

```python
        data = list(reader)

    total_age = sum(int(row[1]) for row in data[1:])
    total_grade = sum(float(row[2]) for row in data[1:])
    num_students = len(data) - 1

    average_age = total_age / num_students
    average_grade = total_grade / num_students

    with open(output_file, 'w', newline='') as csv_file:
        writer = csv.writer(csv_file)
        writer.writerow(data[0] + ['Average Age', 'Average Grade'])
        for row in data[1:]:
            writer.writerow(row + [average_age, average_grade])

# Example usage
process_student_data('students.csv', 'processed_students.csv')
```

Explanation:

1. The process_student_data function takes two file paths as input: input_file (the source CSV file) and output_file (the destination CSV file).
2. The function opens the input CSV file using the with statement and the csv.reader function from the csv module. It reads the data into a list of lists (data).
3. The function calculates the total age and total grade of all students by iterating over the rows (excluding the header row) and summing the age and grade values.
4. The number of students is calculated by subtracting 1 from the length of the data list (to exclude the header row).
5. The average age and average grade are calculated by dividing the total age and total grade by the number of students, respectively.
6. The function opens the output CSV file using the with statement and the csv.writer function from the csv module.
7. It writes the header row, which includes the original columns (name, age, grade) and two additional columns for the average age and average grade.
8. For each row in the original data (excluding the header row), the function writes a new row to the output file, appending the average age and average grade values.

Note: Make sure to have a CSV file named students.csv in the same directory as your Python script for the CSV File Processing project to work correctly. The students.csv file should have the following format:

```
Name,Age,Grade
John Doe,20,85.5
Jane Smith,22,92.0
Bob Johnson,19,78.0
...
```

Chapter 6: Object-Oriented Programming (OOP)

6.1 Introduction to Object-Oriented Programming (OOP) in Python

In the world of computer programming, Python has emerged as a powerful and versatile language, embraced by developers across various domains. One of the key features that contribute to Python's popularity is its strong support for Object-Oriented Programming (OOP). OOP is a programming paradigm that revolves around the creation and manipulation of objects, which encapsulate data and behavior within a single entity.

6.2 Python Classes and Objects

In the realm of object-oriented programming (OOP), classes and objects form the foundational building blocks that enable the creation of modular, reusable, and scalable code. Python, a versatile and widely adopted programming language, provides robust support for OOP concepts, making it an excellent choice for developers to embrace this paradigm. This article aims to introduce absolute beginners to the concepts of classes and objects in Python, laying the groundwork for an in-depth understanding and effective implementation of OOP principles.

Understanding Classes

In Python, a class is a blueprint or template that defines the characteristics and behaviors of objects. It serves as a blueprint for creating objects, specifying their attributes (data) and methods (functions). Classes encapsulate data and functionality, promoting code organization, reusability, and maintainability.

Here's an example of a simple Python class definition:

```python
class Car:
    def __init__(self, make, model, year):
        self.make = make
        self.model = model
        self.year = year

    def display_info(self):
        print(f"Make: {self.make}, Model: {self.model}, Year: {self.year}")
```

In this example, the `Car` class has three attributes (`make`, `model`, and `year`), as well as a method `display_info()`. The `__init__` method is a special method in Python classes, known as the constructor, which is automatically called when an object is created from the class. It initializes the object's attributes with the provided values.

Creating Objects

Once a class is defined, you can create instances of that class, which are called objects. Objects are the actual representations of the class, containing their own set of attributes and methods as defined by the class.

To create an object in Python, you simply call the class name as if it were a function, passing any required arguments to the constructor:

```python
car1 = Car("Toyota", "Camry", 2020)
car2 = Car("Honda", "Civic", 2018)
```

In this example, `car1` and `car2` are objects (instances) of the `Car` class, each with their own unique values for the `make`, `model`, and `year` attributes.

Accessing Object Attributes and Methods

After creating objects, you can access and manipulate their attributes and call their methods using the dot notation:

```python
print(car1.make)   # Output: Toyota
print(car2.model)  # Output: Civic

car1.display_info()  # Output: Make: Toyota, Model: Camry, Year: 2020
car2.display_info()  # Output: Make: Honda, Model: Civic, Year: 2018
```

In the example above, we access the `make` and `model` attributes of `car1` and `car2` using the dot notation (`object.attribute`). Additionally, we call the `display_info()` method on both objects to print their information.

Constructors and Instance Attributes

In Python, the `__init__` method is a special constructor method that is automatically called when an object is created from a class. It is used to initialize the object's attributes with the provided values.

```python
class Car:
    def __init__(self, make, model, year):
        self.make = make
        self.model = model
        self.year = year
        self.odometer = 0  # Initialize odometer to 0
```

In this example, we've added an `odometer` attribute to the `Car` class and initialized it to `0` in the `__init__` method. Each instance of the `Car` class will have its own `odometer` attribute with an initial value of `0`.

Instance Methods

Instance methods are functions defined within a class that operate on the instance (object) of the class. They have access to the object's attributes and can modify them or perform operations based on the object's state.

```python
class Car:
    def __init__(self, make, model, year):
        self.make = make
        self.model = model
        self.year = year
        self.odometer = 0

    def update_odometer(self, mileage):
        self.odometer += mileage

car1 = Car("Toyota", "Camry", 2020)
print(car1.odometer)   # Output: 0

car1.update_odometer(100)
print(car1.odometer)   # Output: 100
```

In this example, we've added an `update_odometer()` method to the `Car` class. This method takes a `mileage` parameter and updates the `odometer` attribute of the object by adding the provided mileage. When we call `car1.update_odometer(100)`, the `odometer` attribute of `car1` is incremented by `100`.

Inheritance

Inheritance is a fundamental concept in OOP that allows a new class (derived or child class) to inherit attributes and methods from an existing class (base or parent class). This promotes code reuse and enables the creation of hierarchical relationships between classes.

```python
class ElectricCar(Car):
    def __init__(self, make, model, year, battery_capacity):
        super().__init__(make, model, year)
        self.battery_capacity = battery_capacity

    def display_battery_info(self):
        print(f"Battery Capacity: {self.battery_capacity} kWh")

car1 = ElectricCar("Tesla", "Model S", 2022, 100)
car1.display_info()         # Output: Make: Tesla, Model: Model S, Year: 2022
car1.display_battery_info() # Output: Battery Capacity: 100 kWh
```

```
```

In this example, we've defined an `ElectricCar` class that inherits from the `Car` class. The `ElectricCar` class has an additional attribute `battery_capacity` and a new method `display_battery_info()`. The `__init__` method of `ElectricCar` calls the `__init__` method of the parent class (`Car`) using the `super().__init__` syntax to initialize the inherited attributes (`make`, `model`, and `year`).

Encapsulation and Access Control

Encapsulation is a principle of OOP that combines data and methods into a single unit (class) and controls access to the class members. Python provides mechanisms for controlling access to class attributes and methods through the use of naming conventions and decorators.

```python
class BankAccount:
    def __init__(self, account_number, balance):
        self._account_number = account_number  # Protected attribute
        self.__balance = balance                # Private attribute

    def deposit(self, amount):
        self.__balance += amount

    def withdraw(self, amount):
        if amount <= self.__balance:
            self.__balance -= amount
        else:
            print("Insufficient funds.")

    def get_balance(self):
        return self.__balance
```

In this example, the `BankAccount` class has two attributes: `_account_number` (protected) and `__balance` (private). The single underscore `_` prefix is a naming convention indicating that the attribute should be treated as protected and can be accessed from within the class or its subclasses. The double underscore `__` prefix is a naming convention indicating that the attribute is private and should not be accessed directly from outside the class.

The `deposit()` and `withdraw()` methods are used to modify the `__balance` attribute, while the `get_balance()` method provides a way to access the `__balance` attribute from outside the class.

Best Practices and Conventions

When working with classes and objects in Python, it's important to follow best practices and conventions to ensure code clarity, maintainability, and consistency. Here are some guidelines to keep in mind:

1. Naming Conventions: Follow the Python naming conventions for classes (UpperCamelCase) and methods/attributes (snake_case). For example, `class MyClass`, `def my_method(self)`, and `self.my_attribute`.

2. Docstrings: Use docstrings (triple-quoted strings) to document your classes, methods, and functions. Docstrings provide a concise description of what the code does and how to use it.

3. Self Parameter: In Python, the first argument of a method is conventionally named `self`, which represents the instance (object) on which the method is called.

4. Encapsulation and Access Control: Use appropriate naming conventions (`_` for protected, `__` for private) to control access to class attributes and methods. Provide getter and setter methods to access and modify private attributes, if necessary.

5. Inheritance and Polymorphism: Leverage inheritance to create hierarchical relationships between classes and promote code reuse. Implement polymorphism by overriding methods in derived classes to provide custom behavior.

6. Testing: Write unit tests for your classes and methods to ensure they function as expected and to catch regressions during future code changes.

7. Code Organization: Organize your classes into modules and packages to promote code reusability and maintainability. Follow the Python module and package conventions for naming and structure.

6.3 Inheritance and Polymorphism

In the realm of object-oriented programming (OOP), inheritance and polymorphism are two fundamental concepts that enable code reuse, extensibility, and flexibility. Python, a versatile and widely adopted programming language, provides robust support for these concepts, allowing developers to create modular, maintainable, and scalable applications. This article aims to introduce absolute beginners to the concepts of inheritance and polymorphism in Python, laying the foundation for effective implementation of OOP principles.

Understanding Inheritance

Inheritance is a mechanism that allows a new class (derived or child class) to inherit attributes and methods from an existing class (base or parent class). This promotes code reuse by enabling the creation of hierarchical relationships between classes, where the derived class inherits and extends the functionality of the base class.

In Python, you can create a derived class by specifying the base class in parentheses when defining the new class:

```python
class Animal:
    def __init__(self, name):
        self.name = name
```

```python
    def speak(self):
        print("The animal makes a sound.")

class Dog(Animal):
    def __init__(self, name, breed):
        super().__init__(name)
        self.breed = breed

    def speak(self):
        print("The dog barks.")

class Cat(Animal):
    def speak(self):
        print("The cat meows.")
```

In this example, the `Dog` and `Cat` classes are derived from the base class `Animal`. The `Dog` class inherits the `name` attribute and the `speak()` method from `Animal`, but also adds a new `breed` attribute and overrides the `speak()` method with its own implementation. The `Cat` class inherits the `name` attribute from `Animal` but overrides the `speak()` method with a different implementation.

To create an instance of a derived class, you can use the same syntax as creating an instance of a base class:

```python
animal = Animal("Generic Animal")
animal.speak()  # Output: The animal makes a sound.

dog = Dog("Buddy", "Labrador")
dog.speak()  # Output: The dog barks.

cat = Cat("Whiskers")
cat.speak()  # Output: The cat meows.
```

In this example, we create instances of the `Animal`, `Dog`, and `Cat` classes and call their respective `speak()` methods. The output demonstrates how the derived classes (`Dog` and `Cat`) have inherited and overridden the behavior of the base class (`Animal`).

Understanding Polymorphism

Polymorphism is the ability of objects to take on many forms. In Python, polymorphism is achieved through method overriding, where a derived class provides its own implementation of a method inherited from its base class.

Polymorphism allows objects of different classes to be treated uniformly, as long as they share a common interface (i.e., methods with the same name and signature). This promotes code flexibility and extensibility, as you can write code that operates on objects of a base class, and the appropriate method implementation will be called based on the actual object type at runtime.

Building upon the previous example, let's explore polymorphism:

```python
def animal_speak(animal):
    animal.speak()

animal_speak(animal)    # Output: The animal makes a sound.
animal_speak(dog)       # Output: The dog barks.
animal_speak(cat)       # Output: The cat meows.
```

In this example, the `animal_speak()` function takes an `animal` parameter and calls its `speak()` method. When we pass instances of the `Animal`, `Dog`, and `Cat` classes to this function, the appropriate implementation of the `speak()` method is called based on the actual object type at runtime. This demonstrates polymorphism, where objects of different classes can be treated uniformly through a common interface (`speak()` method).

Advantages of Inheritance and Polymorphism

Incorporating inheritance and polymorphism into your Python projects offers several advantages:

1. Code Reuse: Inheritance allows you to reuse existing code by inheriting attributes and methods from base classes, reducing duplication and promoting code maintainability.

2. Extensibility: Derived classes can extend the functionality of base classes by adding new attributes and methods or overriding existing ones. This enables the creation of specialized classes while leveraging the existing code.

3. Flexibility: Polymorphism allows objects of different classes to be treated uniformly through a common interface, promoting code flexibility and extensibility.

4. Abstraction: Inheritance and polymorphism support the principle of abstraction, which helps to hide implementation details and expose only the necessary interfaces, making code easier to understand and maintain.

5. Code Organization: Inheritance promotes the organization of code into hierarchical structures, enabling better code organization and modeling of real-world relationships between classes.

Best Practices and Considerations

While inheritance and polymorphism are powerful concepts, it's important to follow best practices and consider potential pitfalls when working with them in Python:

1. Favor Composition over Inheritance: In some cases, composition (creating objects that contain other objects) may be a better design choice than inheritance, as it can promote code reuse and flexibility without the potential issues of complex inheritance hierarchies.

2. Avoid Deep Inheritance Hierarchies: Deep inheritance hierarchies can make code harder to understand and maintain. Aim for shallow hierarchies and consider alternative design patterns, such as composition or delegation, when appropriate.

3. Ensure Method Compatibility: When overriding methods in derived classes, ensure that the new implementations are compatible with the base class implementation in terms of method signatures and expected behavior.

4. Document Inheritance Relationships: Clearly document the inheritance relationships between classes, as well as the intended behavior and responsibilities of each class, to facilitate code maintainability and collaboration.

5. Test Thoroughly: As with any code, it's crucial to write comprehensive unit tests to ensure the correctness of your classes, inheritance relationships, and polymorphic behavior.

6. Consider Performance Implications: While Python's dynamic nature allows for polymorphism, method dispatching at runtime can have performance implications in certain scenarios. Be mindful of potential performance bottlenecks and optimize your code accordingly.

6.4 Special Methods and Operator Overloading

In the realm of object-oriented programming (OOP), Python offers a powerful feature that allows developers to customize the behavior of objects and classes. This feature, known as special methods or magic methods, provides a way to define how objects should behave in response to various operators and built-in functions. One of the most notable applications of special methods is operator overloading, which enables you to define how operators (such as +, -, *, /, etc.) should work with objects of your custom classes. This article aims to introduce absolute beginners to the concepts of special methods and operator overloading in Python, enabling them to unlock the full potential of OOP and create more expressive and intuitive code.

Special methods, also known as magic methods or dunder methods (short for "double underscore"), are predefined methods in Python that have special names and behaviors. These methods are surrounded by double underscores, such as `__init__` and `__str__`. Python automatically invokes these methods in specific situations, allowing you to customize the behavior of your objects and classes.

Here are some commonly used special methods in Python:

1. `__init__(self, ...):` This method is the constructor for a class and is called when an object of the class is created. It is used to initialize the object's attributes.

2. `__str__(self):` This method is called when you try to convert an object to a string representation, such as when using the `print()` function or string formatting operations.

3. `__len__(self):` This method is called when you try to get the length of an object, such as when using the `len()` function.

4. `__add__(self, other):` This method is called when you use the `+` operator on an object.

5. `__mul__(self, other):` This method is called when you use the `*` operator on an object.

These are just a few examples of special methods in Python. There are many more special methods available, each serving a specific purpose and allowing you to customize various aspects of object behavior.

Operator Overloading

Operator overloading is a feature in Python that allows you to define how operators should work with objects of your custom classes. By implementing special methods, you can overload operators to perform custom operations on your objects, making your code more expressive and intuitive.

Let's consider an example where we create a `Vector` class and overload the `+` and `*` operators to perform vector addition and scalar multiplication, respectively:

```python
class Vector:
    def __init__(self, x, y):
        self.x = x
        self.y = y

    def __str__(self):
        return f"Vector({self.x}, {self.y})"

    def __add__(self, other):
        return Vector(self.x + other.x, self.y + other.y)

    def __mul__(self, scalar):
        return Vector(self.x * scalar, self.y * scalar)

# Creating and using Vector objects
v1 = Vector(2, 3)
v2 = Vector(4, 5)
v3 = v1 + v2   # Calls __add__() method
print(v3)      # Output: Vector(6, 8)

v4 = v1 * 2    # Calls __mul__() method
print(v4)      # Output: Vector(4, 6)
```

In this example, we define the `Vector` class with the `__init__` method to initialize the `x` and `y` components of a vector. We also implement the `__str__` method to provide a string representation of the vector.

To enable vector addition, we define the `__add__` method, which takes another `Vector` object (`other`) and returns a new `Vector` object with the sum of the corresponding components.

For scalar multiplication, we define the `__mul__` method, which takes a scalar value and returns a new `Vector` object with each component multiplied by the scalar.

By overloading the `+` and `*` operators using the `__add__` and `__mul__` methods, respectively, we can perform vector operations using the familiar mathematical notation, making our code more readable and expressive.

Benefits of Special Methods and Operator Overloading

Incorporating special methods and operator overloading into your Python projects offers several advantages:

1. Expressive and Intuitive Code: Operator overloading allows you to define custom behavior for operators, making your code more expressive and intuitive, especially when working with custom data types or mathematical operations.

2. Code Reuse and Consistency: By overloading operators and implementing special methods, you can ensure consistent behavior across your code, promoting code reuse and maintainability.

3. Integration with Built-in Functions and Operators: Special methods enable your custom classes to work seamlessly with built-in Python functions and operators, providing a more natural and integrated experience.

4. Improved Readability: When used judiciously, operator overloading can improve code readability by making complex operations more concise and easier to understand.

Best Practices and Considerations

While special methods and operator overloading are powerful features in Python, it's important to follow best practices and consider potential pitfalls when working with them:

1. Follow Established Conventions: When overloading operators or implementing special methods, follow the established conventions and ensure that your implementation aligns with the expected behavior of the operator or method.

2. Maintain Operator Consistency: Ensure that the behavior of overloaded operators is consistent with their mathematical or logical counterparts. Avoid introducing surprising or counterintuitive behavior.

3. Document Custom Behavior: Clearly document the custom behavior of overloaded operators and special methods in your code to facilitate code maintainability and collaboration.

4. Avoid Overuse: While operator overloading can improve code readability, overusing it can lead to obscure and difficult-to-understand code. Use it judiciously and prioritize clarity over conciseness.

5. Test Thoroughly: As with any code, it's crucial to write comprehensive unit tests to ensure the correctness of your special method implementations and operator overloading behavior.

6. Consider Performance Implications: While Python's dynamic nature allows for operator overloading and special methods, be mindful of potential performance implications, especially in computationally intensive scenarios.

Exercise: Bank Account

Create a BankAccount class that has the following methods:
- __init__(self, account_number, balance): Initializes a new bank account with an account number and an initial balance.
- deposit(self, amount): Adds the specified amount to the account balance.
- withdraw(self, amount): Subtracts the specified amount from the account balance if there are sufficient funds; otherwise, it raises an InsufficientFundsError.
- check_balance(self): Returns the current account balance.

Additionally, create a custom exception class called InsufficientFundsError that inherits from the base Exception class.

Solution:

```python
class InsufficientFundsError(Exception):
    """Raised when there are insufficient funds in the account"""
    pass

class BankAccount:
    def __init__(self, account_number, balance):
        self.account_number = account_number
        self.balance = balance

    def deposit(self, amount):
        self.balance += amount
        print(f"Deposited ${amount} into account {self.account_number}")

    def withdraw(self, amount):
        if self.balance < amount:
            raise InsufficientFundsError(f"Insufficient funds in account
{self.account_number}")
        self.balance -= amount
        print(f"Withdrew ${amount} from account {self.account_number}")

    def check_balance(self):
        print(f"Balance of account {self.account_number}: ${self.balance}")

# Example usage
account = BankAccount("123456789", 1000)
account.check_balance()   # Balance of account 123456789: $1000.0
```

```
account.deposit(500)   # Deposited $500 into account 123456789
account.check_balance()   # Balance of account 123456789: $1500.0

try:
    account.withdraw(2000)
except InsufficientFundsError as e:
    print(e)   # Insufficient funds in account 123456789

account.withdraw(1000)   # Withdrew $1000 from account 123456789
account.check_balance()   # Balance of account 123456789: $500.0
```

Explanation:

1. The InsufficientFundsError class is defined as a custom exception that inherits from the base Exception class.
2. The BankAccount class is defined with an __init__ method that initializes a new bank account with an account number and an initial balance.
3. The deposit method adds the specified amount to the account balance and prints a message.
4. The withdraw method first checks if the account balance is sufficient to cover the withdrawal amount. If not, it raises an InsufficientFundsError with an appropriate error message. If the funds are available, it subtracts the amount from the account balance and prints a message.
5. The check_balance method simply prints the current account balance.
6. In the example usage, a new BankAccount object is created with an account number and an initial balance of $1000.
7. The check_balance method is called to display the initial balance.
8. The deposit method is called to add $500 to the account balance, and the new balance is displayed.
9. The withdraw method is called with an amount greater than the account balance, which raises an InsufficientFundsError. The error is caught and printed.
10. The withdraw method is called with a valid amount, and the new balance is displayed.

Project: Geometric Shapes

Create a base class called Shape and derived classes for specific shapes like Rectangle, Circle, and Triangle. Each shape class should have methods to calculate its area and perimeter (or circumference for circles). Implement polymorphism by creating a function that takes a list of shapes and calculates the total area of all shapes.

Solution:

```
import math

class Shape:
    def area(self):
        raise NotImplementedError("Area method not implemented in base
class")

    def perimeter(self):
```

```python
        raise NotImplementedError("Perimeter method not implemented in base
class")

class Rectangle(Shape):
    def __init__(self, length, width):
        self.length = length
        self.width = width

    def area(self):
        return self.length * self.width

    def perimeter(self):
        return 2 * (self.length + self.width)

class Circle(Shape):
    def __init__(self, radius):
        self.radius = radius

    def area(self):
        return math.pi * self.radius ** 2

    def perimeter(self):
        return 2 * math.pi * self.radius

class Triangle(Shape):
    def __init__(self, base, height):
        self.base = base
        self.height = height

    def area(self):
        return 0.5 * self.base * self.height

    def perimeter(self):
        # Assuming a right-angled triangle
        hypotenuse = (self.base ** 2 + self.height ** 2) ** 0.5
        return self.base + self.height + hypotenuse

def total_area(shapes):
    total = 0
    for shape in shapes:
        total += shape.area()
    return total

# Example usage
shapes = [
    Rectangle(5, 10),
    Circle(7),
    Triangle(3, 4)
]
```

```
for shape in shapes:
    print(f"{type(shape).__name__}: Area = {shape.area()}, Perimeter =
{shape.perimeter()}")

print(f"Total area of all shapes: {total_area(shapes)}")
```

Explanation:

1. The Shape class is defined as a base class with abstract methods area and perimeter that raise a NotImplementedError.
2. The Rectangle class inherits from Shape and implements the area and perimeter methods for rectangles.
3. The Circle class inherits from Shape and implements the area and perimeter (circumference) methods for circles, using the math module for calculations involving π.
4. The Triangle class inherits from Shape and implements the area and perimeter methods for right-angled triangles.
5. The total_area function takes a list of Shape objects and calculates the total area by calling the area method on each shape and summing the results.
6. In the example usage, a list of shapes (rectangle, circle, and triangle) is created.
7. A for loop iterates over the list of shapes, prints the type of each shape, its area, and its perimeter (or circumference for circles).
8. Finally, the total_area function is called with the list of shapes, and the total area is printed.

Chapter 7: Exception handling

Exception handling is a crucial aspect of writing robust and reliable Python code. It allows you to gracefully handle errors, prevent program crashes, and ensure that unexpected situations are managed effectively. Let's explore the key concepts related to exception handling in Python:

7.1 Understanding Exceptions

In the realm of computer programming, exceptions play a crucial role in ensuring the robustness and reliability of software applications. Exceptions are events that occur during program execution, disrupting the normal flow of instructions and potentially causing the program to terminate unexpectedly. Understanding exceptions is a fundamental concept for developers, as it enables them to anticipate and handle errors gracefully, providing a better user experience and preventing data loss or system crashes.

This comprehensive guide aims to introduce absolute beginners to the concept of exceptions, covering essential topics such as what exceptions are, why they occur, how to handle them, and best practices for effective exception management. By mastering these concepts, beginners will be equipped with the knowledge and skills necessary to write robust and resilient code, capable of handling unexpected situations and delivering a seamless user experience.

What are Exceptions?

Exceptions are unexpected events or conditions that occur during program execution, which deviate from the normal flow of instructions. They can be caused by various factors, such as invalid user input, file access issues, network connectivity problems, or programming errors (e.g., dividing by zero, accessing an out-of-bounds index in a list, or attempting to use an uninitialized variable).

In most programming languages, when an exception occurs, the normal execution of the program is interrupted, and the control is transferred to an exception handling mechanism. If the exception is not handled properly, it can lead to program termination, potential data loss, or system crashes.

Why Do Exceptions Occur?

Exceptions can occur for a multitude of reasons, ranging from programming errors to external factors beyond the control of the application. Here are some common scenarios where exceptions may arise:

1. Programming Errors: Logical errors or mistakes in the code can lead to exceptions, such as attempting to access an out-of-bounds index in a list, dividing by zero, or using an uninitialized variable.

2. Invalid User Input: When an application receives invalid or unexpected user input, it can trigger exceptions. For example, attempting to convert a non-numeric string to an integer or attempting to open a file that does not exist.

3. Resource Unavailability: Exceptions can occur when an application fails to access or utilize required resources, such as files, network connections, or external services.

4. System Errors: Hardware failures, operating system issues, or other system-level problems can cause exceptions to be raised within an application.

5. Third-Party Libraries or APIs: When an application integrates with third-party libraries or APIs, exceptions can occur due to compatibility issues, version conflicts, or errors within those external components.

By understanding the potential sources of exceptions, developers can better anticipate and handle these situations, ensuring a more robust and reliable application.

7.2 Try-Except Blocks

In the realm of computer programming, exceptions are an inevitable part of the software development process. Regardless of how well-designed and thoroughly tested a program may be, there is always a possibility of encountering unexpected situations or errors during execution. To ensure that applications handle these exceptional circumstances gracefully and continue to operate as intended, most programming languages provide mechanisms for exception handling. One of the most widely used and fundamental constructs for exception handling is the try-except block.

This comprehensive guide aims to introduce absolute beginners to the concept of try-except blocks, exploring their purpose, syntax, and various applications across different programming languages. By understanding the significance and proper usage of try-except blocks, beginners will be equipped with the knowledge and skills necessary to write robust, reliable, and user-friendly code that can effectively handle and recover from exceptional situations.

Understanding Exceptions

Before delving into the intricacies of try-except blocks, it is essential to understand the concept of exceptions. Exceptions are events or conditions that occur during program execution, disrupting the normal flow of instructions and potentially causing the program to terminate unexpectedly. These exceptional situations can arise due to various reasons, such as programming errors (e.g., dividing by zero, accessing an out-of-bounds index in a list), invalid user input, file access issues, network connectivity problems, or system-level errors.

When an exception occurs, it is typically represented by an exception object that encapsulates information about the error, such as an error message, error code, and other relevant details. If an exception is not handled properly, it can lead to program termination, potential data loss, or system crashes, resulting in an undesirable user experience and potential data integrity issues.

The Role of Try-Except Blocks

Try-except blocks provide a structured way to anticipate and handle exceptions within a program. They allow developers to define a section of code where exceptions might occur (the "try" block) and specify how to handle those exceptions (the "except" block). By enclosing potentially problematic code within a try block and providing corresponding exception handlers in the except block(s), developers can gracefully recover from exceptional situations, take appropriate actions, and prevent program termination.

The Basic Syntax of Try-Except Blocks

While the specific syntax for try-except blocks may vary slightly across programming languages, the general structure follows a common pattern:

```
try:
    # Code that might raise an exception
    # ...
except Exception1:
    # Code to handle Exception1
    # ...
except Exception2:
    # Code to handle Exception2
    # ...
# Optional additional exception handlers
# ...
# Optional "else" block
# ...
# Optional "finally" block
# ...
```

Here's a breakdown of the different components of a try-except block:

1. Try Block: This is the section of code where potentially problematic operations are performed. If an exception occurs within this block, the program's execution is immediately transferred to the corresponding except block that handles that specific type of exception.

2. Except Block(s): These blocks define the exception handlers, specifying the types of exceptions to catch and the actions to take when those exceptions are raised. Each except block is responsible for handling a specific type of exception or a group of related exceptions.

3. Else Block (Optional): In some programming languages, an optional "else" block can be included after the except block(s). The code within the else block is executed only if no exceptions were raised in the try block.

4. Finally Block (Optional): Some languages also provide an optional "finally" block, which contains code that will be executed regardless of whether an exception occurred or not. This block is typically used for cleanup operations, such as closing files, releasing resources, or performing any necessary finalization tasks.

By structuring exception handling code within try-except blocks, developers can organize their code in a clear and readable manner, making it easier to understand and maintain.

Handling Exceptions with Try-Except Blocks

To illustrate the usage of try-except blocks, let's consider an example in Python, a popular programming language known for its readability and simplicity:

```python
try:
    numerator = int(input("Enter the numerator: "))
    denominator = int(input("Enter the denominator: "))
    result = numerator / denominator
    print(f"The result is: {result}")
except ValueError:
    print("Error: Invalid input. Please enter numeric values.")
except ZeroDivisionError:
    print("Error: Cannot divide by zero.")
except Exception as e:
    print(f"An unexpected error occurred: {e}")
else:
    print("Division completed successfully.")
finally:
    print("This message will be printed regardless of exceptions.")
```

In this example, we have a program that prompts the user to enter a numerator and a denominator, performs division on these values, and prints the result. However, there are several potential exceptions that can occur during the execution of this code:

1. ValueError: This exception can be raised if the user enters non-numeric values for the numerator or denominator.
2. ZeroDivisionError: This exception occurs when attempting to divide a number by zero, which is an invalid operation.
3. Other Exceptions: There may be other unexpected exceptions that could occur, such as memory errors or system-level errors.

To handle these exceptions, we use a try-except block structure:

- The `try` block contains the code that might raise an exception, including the user input prompts, value conversions, and the division operation.
- The first `except` block handles the `ValueError` exception by printing an error message about invalid input.
- The second `except` block handles the `ZeroDivisionError` exception by printing an error message about dividing by zero.
- The third `except` block catches all other exceptions (specified as `Exception` in Python) and prints a generic error message.
- The `else` block is executed if no exceptions were raised in the `try` block, indicating that the division operation completed successfully.
- The `finally` block contains code that will always be executed, regardless of whether an exception occurred or not. In this case, it prints a message confirming that the program reached this point.

By using try-except blocks, this program can gracefully handle various exceptional situations, providing informative error messages to the user and preventing the program from terminating unexpectedly.

Exception Hierarchies and Catching Multiple Exceptions

Many programming languages organize exceptions into hierarchical structures, with specific exception types inheriting from more general ones. This hierarchical structure allows developers to catch and handle exceptions at appropriate levels, either by catching specific exception types or by catching broader categories of exceptions.

For example, in Python, the `Exception` class is the base class for all built-in exceptions, and more specific exception types inherit from it. By catching the `Exception` class, you can handle any type of exception that might occur in your code. However, it is generally recommended to catch specific exception types whenever possible, as this provides more targeted and meaningful exception handling.

Some programming languages also allow you to catch multiple exception types in a single except block, using a tuple or other syntax constructs. Here's an example in Python:

```python
try:
    # Code that might raise exceptions
    # ...
except (ValueError, TypeError):
    # Code to handle ValueError or TypeError
    # ...
```

In this example, the `except` block catches both `ValueError` and `TypeError` exceptions, allowing you to handle them together with the same exception handling code.

Best Practices for Using Try-Except Blocks

While try-except blocks are powerful tools for exception handling, it is essential to follow best practices to ensure effective and maintainable code:

1. Catch Specific Exceptions: Instead of catching broad, general exceptions (e.g., `Exception` in Python), it is recommended to catch specific exception types that are relevant to your code. This approach provides better clarity and allows for more targeted exception handling.

2. Provide Informative Error Messages: When handling exceptions, provide clear and informative error messages that help users or developers understand the cause of the error and potentially resolve the issue.

3. Implement Proper Error Handling and Logging: In addition to displaying error messages, consider implementing error logging mechanisms to capture and record exception details for future analysis and debugging.

4. Avoid Catching Broad Exceptions Unnecessarily: While it is sometimes necessary to catch broad exceptions (e.g., `Exception` in Python) to prevent program termination, avoid doing so unnecessarily, as it can mask other exceptions and make it harder to diagnose and fix issues.

5. Clean Up Resources in `finally` Blocks: Use `finally` blocks to ensure that resources (e.g., file handles, network connections, database connections) are properly cleaned up or released, regardless of whether an exception occurred or not.

6. Propagate Exceptions When Appropriate: In some cases, it may be appropriate to propagate exceptions up the call stack, allowing higher-level components or modules to handle the exception more appropriately.

7. Document Exception Handling Strategies: Document your exception handling strategies, including the types of exceptions caught, the actions taken, and any relevant assumptions or dependencies.

8. Test Exception Handling Code: Ensure that your exception handling code is thoroughly tested, including edge cases and scenarios that trigger different types of exceptions.

9. Consider Exception Hierarchies: When working with complex exception hierarchies, consider the relationships and inheritance structures to ensure proper exception handling and propagation.

10. Embrace Defensive Programming: Adopt a defensive programming mindset, anticipating and handling potential exceptions proactively, rather than reactively addressing issues as they arise.

By following these best practices, developers can create more robust, maintainable, and user-friendly applications that gracefully handle exceptional situations, providing a better overall experience for users and enabling easier troubleshooting and debugging.

Advanced Topics and Language-Specific Considerations

While the core concepts of try-except blocks are consistent across programming languages, there may be language-specific features, syntax variations, and advanced topics to consider. Here are some examples:

1. Raising Exceptions: Many programming languages provide mechanisms for explicitly raising or throwing exceptions when specific conditions are met. This allows developers to create and propagate custom exceptions tailored to their application's needs.

2. Exception Hierarchies and Custom Exceptions: Some languages offer the ability to create custom exception types and organize them into hierarchical structures, enabling more fine-grained exception handling and inheritance relationships.

3. Multiple Exception Handling: Some languages support catching multiple exceptions in a single except block, either by specifying a tuple of exception types or using other syntax constructs.

4. Context Managers (with Statement): In languages like Python, context managers (implemented using the `with` statement) provide a convenient and safer way to handle resources that require explicit setup and teardown, such as file operations or database connections.

5. Exception Filters and Guards: Certain programming languages allow developers to specify additional conditions or filters within except blocks, enabling more granular exception handling based on specific criteria or exception properties.

6. Exception Chaining and Nested Exceptions: Some languages support exception chaining or nested exceptions, where an exception can encapsulate and propagate another exception, providing valuable context and information for debugging and error handling.

7. Language-Specific Exception Handling Idioms and Conventions: Each programming language may have its own idioms, conventions, and best practices for exception handling, which developers should be aware of and follow to ensure consistent and maintainable code.

As you delve deeper into exception handling and try-except blocks in your programming language of choice, it is essential to consult the language's official documentation, style guides, and community resources to gain a comprehensive understanding of language-specific features, advanced topics, and best practices.

7.3 Raising Exceptions

In the world of programming, exceptional situations or errors can occur during the execution of a program. These exceptional conditions, also known as exceptions, can arise due to various reasons, such as invalid user input, file access issues, network connectivity problems, or even programming logic errors. When an exception occurs, it disrupts the normal flow of the program's execution, which can lead to unexpected behavior or even crashes.

Python, like many modern programming languages, provides a robust exception handling mechanism that allows you to gracefully handle exceptional situations and prevent your program from crashing. One essential aspect of exception handling in Python is the ability to raise (or throw) exceptions from within your code. Raising exceptions is a powerful tool that enables you to signal and communicate exceptional conditions, making it easier to write more robust and maintainable code.

Before delving into raising exceptions, it's crucial to understand what exceptions are and how they work in Python. An exception is an object that represents an error or exceptional condition that has occurred during the execution of a program. When an exception is raised, it interrupts the normal flow of the program's execution, and the program enters an exceptional state.

Python provides a rich hierarchy of built-in exception classes, each representing a specific type of exception. These classes are derived from the base `Exception` class, and they are organized in a hierarchical structure. For example, `ValueError` is a subclass of `Exception` and is raised when an operation receives an argument of an inappropriate type or value. Similarly, `FileNotFoundError` is a subclass of `OSError` and is raised when a file or directory cannot be found.

Raising Exceptions in Python

In Python, you can raise an exception using the `raise` statement. This statement is typically followed by an instance of an exception class or a call to an exception class constructor. Here's the general syntax for raising an exception:

```python
raise ExceptionClass("Error message")
```

Let's explore a few examples to understand how to raise exceptions in different scenarios.

Example 1: Raising a Built-in Exception

Python provides many built-in exception classes that you can use to raise exceptions in your code. Here's an example that raises a `ValueError` when a function receives an invalid argument:

```python
def divide_numbers(a, b):
    if b == 0:
        raise ValueError("Cannot divide by zero")
    return a / b

try:
    result = divide_numbers(10, 0)
    print(f"Result: {result}")
except ValueError as e:
    print(f"Error: {e}")
```

In this example, the `divide_numbers` function checks if the denominator (`b`) is zero. If it is, the function raises a `ValueError` with an appropriate error message using the `raise` statement. The `try`-`except` block is used to catch and handle the raised exception gracefully.

Example 2: Raising a Custom Exception

While Python provides a rich set of built-in exception classes, there may be times when you need to define and raise your own custom exceptions. Custom exceptions are particularly useful when you want to represent and handle specific error conditions that are unique to your application domain or project.

Here's an example that defines and raises a custom exception:

```python
class InvalidAgeError(Exception):
    """Raised when an invalid age value is encountered."""
    pass

def validate_age(age):
    if age < 0 or age > 120:
        raise InvalidAgeError(f"Invalid age: {age}")
```

```
try:
    validate_age(-5)
except InvalidAgeError as e:
    print(f"Error: {e}")
```

In this example, we define a custom exception class called `InvalidAgeError` that inherits from the base `Exception` class. The `validate_age` function checks if the provided age is within a valid range (0 to 120). If the age is invalid, the function raises an `InvalidAgeError` with an appropriate error message.

When raising a custom exception, you can include additional information or data in the exception object by passing it as an argument to the exception class constructor. This information can be useful for debugging or logging purposes.

Example 3: Raising Exceptions with Context

Python's `raise` statement also supports providing additional context information when raising an exception. This can be particularly helpful when you want to include more details about the exceptional condition or when you need to re-raise an exception after performing additional operations.

Here's an example that demonstrates raising an exception with context:

```python
def divide_numbers(a, b):
    try:
        return a / b
    except ZeroDivisionError as e:
        raise ZeroDivisionError("Cannot divide by zero") from e

try:
    result = divide_numbers(10, 0)
    print(f"Result: {result}")
except ZeroDivisionError as e:
    print(f"Error: {e}")
```

In this example, the `divide_numbers` function attempts to divide two numbers. If a `ZeroDivisionError` occurs (because the denominator is zero), the function re-raises the exception with a custom error message and includes the original exception context using the `from` clause. This allows you to preserve the original traceback information while adding your own error message or context.

Best Practices for Raising Exceptions in Python

While raising exceptions is a powerful tool for error handling and control flow management in Python, it's important to follow best practices to ensure that your code is readable, maintainable, and efficient. Here are some guidelines to keep in mind when raising exceptions:

1. Raise exceptions judiciously: Exceptions should be raised for truly exceptional circumstances, not for regular control flow or expected situations. Overusing exceptions can make your code harder to read and reason about, and can also have performance implications.

2. Provide clear and informative error messages: When raising an exception, include a clear and descriptive error message that explains the nature of the exceptional condition. This will greatly aid in debugging and understanding the cause of the exception.

3. Use appropriate exception types: Choose the most specific and appropriate exception type for the exceptional condition you're handling. This makes your code more self-documenting and easier to maintain.

4. Consider defining custom exception classes: If none of the built-in exception classes adequately represent the exceptional condition in your application domain, consider defining your own custom exception classes. This can improve code readability and make it easier to handle and propagate specific types of exceptions.

5. Catch exceptions at the appropriate level: Catch exceptions at the level where you can effectively handle them. Avoid catching exceptions too broadly or too narrowly, as this can lead to code that is difficult to maintain or debug.

6. Propagate exceptions when necessary: If you cannot handle an exception at the current level, propagate it up the call stack by re-raising the exception or allowing it to bubble up naturally. This allows higher-level code or external exception handlers to handle the exception appropriately.

7. Document exception handling in your code: Clearly document the exceptions that your code can raise, as well as the exceptions that it can handle or propagate. This documentation can be in the form of docstrings, comments, or external documentation.

8. Test exception handling: As part of your testing and quality assurance processes, ensure that you thoroughly test your exception handling code, including raising and catching exceptions in various scenarios.

By following these best practices, you can leverage the power of raising exceptions in Python to write more robust, maintainable, and reliable code that can gracefully handle errors and exceptional situations.

7.4 Custom Exceptions

In Python, exceptions are a fundamental mechanism for handling errors and exceptional situations that may arise during program execution. While Python provides a rich set of built-in exceptions to handle common error scenarios, there are times when you may need to define your own custom exceptions to cater to the specific needs of your application or domain.

Custom exceptions allow you to create more meaningful and descriptive error messages, encapsulate domain-specific logic, and provide a structured way of handling exceptional cases in your code. By defining custom exceptions, you can enhance the readability, maintainability, and extensibility of your Python programs.

In this section, we will delve into the concept of custom exceptions in Python, exploring their creation, usage, and best practices. We will also examine various scenarios where custom exceptions can be beneficial and provide illustrative examples to reinforce the concepts discussed.

Creating Custom Exceptions

In Python, all exceptions are classes that inherit from the base `Exception` class or one of its subclasses. To create a custom exception, you simply need to define a new class that inherits from `Exception` or a more specific built-in exception class.

Here's the basic syntax for creating a custom exception class:

```python
class CustomException(Exception):
    """A custom exception for specific error scenarios."""
    pass
```

In this example, we define a new `CustomException` class that inherits directly from the base `Exception` class. The `pass` statement is used as a placeholder, as the class doesn't have any additional functionality or attributes at this point.

You can also add custom properties, methods, or behavior to your custom exception class, depending on your specific requirements. For instance, you might want to include additional information or metadata related to the exceptional condition:

```python
class InvalidEmailError(Exception):
    """Raised when an invalid email address is provided."""

    def __init__(self, email, message="Invalid email address"):
        self.email = email
        self.message = message
        super().__init__(self.message)

    def __str__(self):
        return f"{self.email} -> {self.message}"
```

In this example, the `InvalidEmailError` class inherits from `Exception` and provides additional functionality:

- The `__init__` method accepts an `email` argument and an optional `message` argument, allowing you to pass in the invalid email address and a custom error message.
- The `__str__` method is overridden to provide a custom string representation of the exception instance, which can be useful for debugging and error reporting purposes.

Raising Custom Exceptions

Once you've defined a custom exception class, you can raise instances of that class using the `raise` statement, just like you would with built-in exceptions.

```python
def validate_email(email):
    # Perform email validation logic
    if not valid_email_pattern.match(email):
        raise InvalidEmailError(email)
    # Continue with other operations

try:
    user_email = input("Enter your email address: ")
    validate_email(user_email)
    print("Email is valid")
except InvalidEmailError as e:
    print(e)
```

In this example, we define a `validate_email` function that checks if the provided email address is valid. If the email is invalid, it raises an `InvalidEmailError` with the email address as an argument. In the `try` block, we call the `validate_email` function with user input, and if the `InvalidEmailError` is raised, we catch it in the `except` block and print the custom error message provided by the `__str__` method.

Exception Hierarchy and Inheritance

Custom exceptions in Python can inherit from any built-in exception class, allowing you to create a hierarchy of exceptions that reflects the relationships and dependencies between different error scenarios. This inheritance model can help you organize and manage exceptions in a more structured and maintainable way.

For example, you might create a base custom exception class for a specific domain or application, and then define more specific exception classes that inherit from that base class:

```python
class ApplicationError(Exception):
    """Base class for all application-specific exceptions."""
    pass

class ConfigurationError(ApplicationError):
    """Raised when there is an error in the application configuration."""
    pass

class DatabaseError(ApplicationError):
    """Raised when there is an error interacting with the database."""
    pass
```

```
```

In this example, we define a base `ApplicationError` class that inherits from `Exception`. We then create two more specific exception classes, `ConfigurationError` and `DatabaseError`, which inherit from `ApplicationError`. This hierarchical structure allows you to handle exceptions at different levels of granularity, depending on your needs.

Exception Chaining

In some cases, you may want to raise a new exception while preserving the context and information from a previously raised exception. This is known as exception chaining, and it helps maintain a clear trail of exceptions that occurred, making it easier to debug and understand the root cause of an error.

To chain exceptions in Python, you can use the `raise` statement with the `from` keyword, followed by the original exception instance. Here's an example:

```python
try:
    num = int(input("Enter a number: "))
except ValueError as e:
    raise InvalidInputError("Invalid input") from e
```

In this example, if the user enters a non-numeric value, a `ValueError` is raised by the `int()` function. We catch this exception in the `except` block and then raise a new `InvalidInputError` with a custom message, while chaining it to the original `ValueError` instance using the `from e` syntax.

Exception chaining is particularly useful when you're working with nested function calls or when you want to provide additional context or error handling logic while preserving the original exception information.

When to Use Custom Exceptions

Custom exceptions can be beneficial in various scenarios, including but not limited to:

- **Domain-specific errors:** When you're working in a specific domain or application area, custom exceptions can help you model and handle errors that are specific to that domain. For example, in a banking application, you might define exceptions like `InsufficientFundsError` or `InvalidTransactionError`.

- **Input validation:** Custom exceptions can be used to handle invalid input scenarios more effectively. Instead of using generic built-in exceptions like `ValueError`, you can create specific exceptions that better describe the nature of the invalid input, such as `InvalidEmailError` or `InvalidPasswordError`.

- **Resource management:** If you're working with external resources like files, databases, or network connections, custom exceptions can help you handle resource-related errors more appropriately. For example, you might define `FilePermissionError` or `NetworkTimeoutError`.

- **Improved code readability and maintainability:** By defining custom exceptions, you can make your code more self-documenting and easier to understand. Well-named custom exceptions provide clear and descriptive error messages, which can aid in debugging and troubleshooting.

- **Separation of concerns:** Custom exceptions can help you separate the error handling logic from the core functionality of your application, promoting better code organization and modularity.

Best Practices for Custom Exceptions

When working with custom exceptions in Python, it's essential to follow best practices to ensure your code is maintainable, readable, and easy to debug. Here are some guidelines to keep in mind:

- **Use descriptive names:** Choose names for your custom exceptions that clearly convey the nature of the exceptional condition or error. Avoid vague or ambiguous names that might cause confusion.

- **Provide informative error messages:** When raising a custom exception, include a clear and informative error message that describes the error and provides enough context for debugging. Avoid generic or uninformative error messages.

- **Document custom exceptions:** If you create custom exceptions, document them thoroughly, including their purpose, when they should be raised, and any additional information or behavior they provide.

- **Follow Python's exception hierarchy:** When defining custom exceptions, consider inheriting from the appropriate built-in exception class or a more specific custom exception class to maintain a logical exception hierarchy.

- **Catch exceptions at the appropriate level:** Catch and handle exceptions at the level where you have enough context and information to handle the error properly. Avoid catching exceptions too broadly or too narrowly.

- **Use exception chaining judiciously:** Exception chaining can be helpful for maintaining context and debugging, but use it judiciously. Excessive chaining or nested exceptions can make your code harder to understand and maintain.

- **Provide consistent behavior:** Ensure that your custom exceptions provide consistent behavior across your codebase. This includes maintaining a consistent method of raising exceptions, handling exceptions, and providing error messages.

- **Test exception handling:** Include test cases to verify that your custom exceptions are raised and handled correctly in various scenarios. This can help ensure the robustness and reliability of your exception handling mechanisms.

Examples and Use Cases

To further illustrate the concept of custom exceptions in Python, let's explore some practical examples and use cases:

Example 1: Raising a custom exception for invalid user input

```python
class InvalidAgeError(ValueError):
    """Raised when an invalid age value is provided."""
    pass

def validate_age(age):
    if age < 0 or age > 120:
        raise InvalidAgeError(f"Age {age} is outside the valid range (0-
120)")
    # Continue with other operations

try:
    validate_age(-5)
except InvalidAgeError as e:
    print(e)
```

In this example, we define a custom `InvalidAgeError` exception that inherits from `ValueError`. The `validate_age` function checks if the provided age is within a valid range (0-120). If the age is invalid, it raises an `InvalidAgeError` with a descriptive error message. In the `try` block, we call the `validate_age` function with an invalid age, and if the exception is raised, we catch it in the `except` block and print the error message.

Example 2: Creating a custom exception hierarchy

```python
class NetworkError(Exception):
    """Base class for network-related exceptions."""
    pass

class ConnectionError(NetworkError):
    """Raised when there is an error connecting to a network resource."""
    pass

class TimeoutError(NetworkError):
    """Raised when a network operation times out."""
    pass

def fetch_data(url, timeout=10):
    # Code to fetch data from a network resource
    if connection_failed:
        raise ConnectionError(f"Failed to connect to {url}")
    elif timed_out:
        raise TimeoutError(f"Connection to {url} timed out after {timeout}
seconds")
    # Continue with other operations
```

```
try:
    fetch_data("https://example.com", timeout=5)
except NetworkError as e:
    print(f"Error: {e}")
```

In this example, we define a custom `NetworkError` exception as the base class for network-related exceptions. We then create two more specific exception classes, `ConnectionError` and `TimeoutError`, which inherit from `NetworkError`. The `fetch_data` function simulates fetching data from a network resource and raises the appropriate exception based on the error scenario (connection failure or timeout). In the `try` block, we call the `fetch_data` function, and if any network-related exception is raised, we catch it in the `except` block using the base `NetworkError` class, allowing us to handle all network-related exceptions in a single block.

Example 3: Exception chaining with custom exceptions

```python
class InvalidInputError(Exception):
    """Raised when the user input is invalid."""
    pass

def get_user_input():
    user_input = input("Enter a number: ")
    try:
        num = int(user_input)
    except ValueError as e:
        raise InvalidInputError("Invalid input") from e
    return num

try:
    result = get_user_input()
    print(f"Result: {result}")
except InvalidInputError as e:
    print(f"Error: {e}")
    print(f"Original error: {e.__cause__}")
```

In this example, we define a custom `InvalidInputError` exception. The `get_user_input` function prompts the user to enter a number and attempts to convert the input to an integer using `int()`. If a `ValueError` is raised during the conversion (e.g., the user entered a non-numeric value), we catch the exception and raise a new `InvalidInputError`, chaining it to the original `ValueError` using the `from e` syntax.

In the `try` block, we call the `get_user_input` function and handle the `InvalidInputError` exception. If the exception is raised, we print the custom error message and the original error message using the `__cause__` attribute of the exception instance, which provides access to the chained exception.

These examples demonstrate how custom exceptions can be used to handle specific error scenarios, create structured exception hierarchies, and provide more meaningful and descriptive error messages. By using custom exceptions effectively, you can enhance the robustness, readability, and maintainability of your Python code.

Exercise: Custom Exception Handling

Create a Python program that simulates a simple banking system. The program should be able to do the following:
1. Allow a user to create an account with an initial deposit.
2. Allow a user to withdraw, deposit, and check the balance.
3. Raise a custom exception InsufficientBalanceException when a user tries to withdraw more than their current balance.

Solution:

```python
class InsufficientBalanceException(Exception):
    pass

class BankAccount:
    def __init__(self, initial_balance):
        self.balance = initial_balance

    def deposit(self, amount):
        self.balance += amount

    def withdraw(self, amount):
        if amount > self.balance:
            raise InsufficientBalanceException("You have insufficient balance
for this transaction.")
        else:
            self.balance -= amount

    def check_balance(self):
        return self.balance

# Create a bank account with an initial balance of 1000
account = BankAccount(1000)

# Deposit 500
account.deposit(500)
print(f"Current balance: {account.check_balance()}")

# Try to withdraw 2000
try:
    account.withdraw(2000)
except InsufficientBalanceException as e:
    print(e)
```

```python
print(f"Current balance: {account.check_balance()}")
```

Explanation

The solution is a simple banking system implemented in Python. It includes a custom exception InsufficientBalanceException and a class BankAccount with methods for depositing, withdrawing, and checking the balance.

1. **Custom Exception - InsufficientBalanceException:** This is a custom exception class that we define. It inherits from the built-in Exception class. We can raise this exception when a specific condition is met - in this case, when a user tries to withdraw more than their current balance.
2. **BankAccount Class:** This class represents a bank account. It has an instance variable balance which is initialized when a BankAccount object is created.
   - **deposit method:** This method takes an amount as an argument and adds it to the current balance.
   - **withdraw method:** This method takes an amount as an argument and subtracts it from the current balance. Before doing so, it checks if the amount is greater than the current balance. If it is, it raises an InsufficientBalanceException.
   - **check_balance method:** This method returns the current balance.
3. **Main Program:** In the main part of the program, we create a BankAccount object with an initial balance of 1000. We then deposit 500 into the account and print the current balance. We try to withdraw 2000 from the account - since this is more than the current balance, our custom InsufficientBalanceException is raised. We catch this exception and print its message. Finally, we print the current balance.

Chapter 8: Practical Projects

Building a Simple Web Scraper in Python

In the age of the internet, where vast amounts of data are readily available on various websites, web scraping has become an increasingly valuable skill for programmers and data enthusiasts alike. Web scraping, also known as web data extraction, involves programmatically retrieving and collecting data from websites. This technique allows you to extract and analyze large datasets that would otherwise be tedious or impossible to gather manually.

Python, with its rich ecosystem of libraries and tools, is an excellent choice for building web scrapers. One of the most popular libraries for web scraping in Python is BeautifulSoup, which provides a simple and intuitive way to parse and navigate HTML and XML documents.

In this chapter, we will walk through the process of building a simple web scraper in Python using the BeautifulSoup library. We'll explore the basic concepts, learn how to set up the necessary tools, and develop a practical example to scrape data from a website.

Understanding Web Scraping

Before diving into the code, let's first understand what web scraping entails. Web scraping involves the following steps:

1. Sending a request to a website to retrieve its HTML or XML content.
2. Parsing the retrieved content to extract the desired data.
3. Optionally, cleaning and structuring the extracted data for further analysis or storage.

Web scraping can be a powerful tool for various applications, such as:

- Price monitoring and comparison
- Market research and competitor analysis
- Data mining and analytics
- Content aggregation and syndication
- Academic research and data collection

However, it's essential to note that web scraping should be done responsibly and ethically, respecting the website's terms of service and avoiding any activities that may cause harm or disrupt the normal operation of the target website.

Setting Up the Environment

To start building our web scraper, we need to set up the necessary tools and libraries. Here's what you'll need:

1. Python: Make sure you have Python installed on your system. You can download the latest version from the official Python website (https://www.python.org/).

2. BeautifulSoup: BeautifulSoup is a Python library for parsing HTML and XML documents. You can install it using pip, the Python package installer:

```
pip install beautifulsoup4
```

3. Requests: The Requests library is used to send HTTP requests and retrieve web content. It can be installed via pip:

```
pip install requests
```

Building the Web Scraper

Now that we have the necessary tools set up, let's dive into building our simple web scraper. We'll use the example of scraping book information from a popular online bookstore website.

Here's the step-by-step process:

1. Import the required libraries:

```python
import requests
from bs4 import BeautifulSoup
```

2. Send a request to the website:

```python
url = "https://www.example.com/books"
response = requests.get(url)
```

In this example, we're using the `requests.get()` function to send an HTTP GET request to the specified URL and retrieve the website's HTML content. The retrieved content is stored in the `response` variable.

3. Parse the HTML content:

```python
soup = BeautifulSoup(response.content, "html.parser")
```

Here, we create a `BeautifulSoup` object by passing the HTML content from the `response` object and specifying the parser to use (`"html.parser"` in this case).

4. Extract the desired data:

```python
book_elements = soup.find_all("div", class_="book-container")

for book in book_elements:
    title = book.find("h3", class_="book-title").text.strip()
    author = book.find("p", class_="book-author").text.strip()
    price = book.find("span", class_="book-price").text.strip()
    print(f"Title: {title}")
    print(f"Author: {author}")
    print(f"Price: {price}")
    print("---")
```

In this step, we use BeautifulSoup's powerful search and navigation methods to extract the desired data from the HTML. We first find all the HTML elements that represent individual book containers using `soup.find_all()`. Then, for each book container, we extract the title, author, and price information by navigating the HTML structure and retrieving the text content of the respective elements.

5. Optional: Save the extracted data:

Depending on your use case, you may want to save the extracted data to a file or a database for further analysis or processing. You can use Python's built-in file handling or database libraries for this purpose.

Best Practices for Web Scraping

While web scraping can be a powerful tool, it's important to follow best practices and ethical guidelines to ensure responsible and sustainable data collection:

1. Respect the website's terms of service: Before scraping a website, review its terms of service and robot exclusion standard (robots.txt) to ensure that web scraping is permitted and within the allowed limits.

2. Implement rate limiting and politeness policies: To avoid overwhelming the target website with excessive requests, implement rate limiting mechanisms and follow politeness policies, such as introducing random delays between requests or respecting the `Retry-After` header.

3. Identify yourself: When sending requests, include a user-agent string that identifies your web scraper and provides contact information in case the website owners need to reach out.

4. Handle errors and exceptions: Implement proper error handling and exception management to gracefully handle situations such as network errors, server timeouts, or changes in the website's structure.

5. Respect data privacy and copyrights: Be mindful of data privacy and intellectual property rights when scraping and using the collected data. Avoid scraping and distributing personal or sensitive information without proper consent.

6. Cache and store data responsibly: If you plan to store the scraped data, ensure that you have appropriate measures in place for data security, privacy, and compliance with relevant regulations.

7. Consider alternative data sources: Evaluate the availability of official APIs or data feeds provided by the website or third-party providers before resorting to web scraping, as these alternatives may be more reliable and sustainable.

By following these best practices, you can ensure that your web scraping activities are responsible, ethical, and sustainable, while minimizing the risk of legal or technical issues.

Creating a Command-Line Tool

In the world of software development, command-line tools play a crucial role in automating tasks, streamlining workflows, and providing a powerful interface for interacting with applications and systems. These tools allow users to execute commands, run scripts, and perform various operations directly from the terminal or command prompt.

Python, with its simplicity and versatility, is an excellent choice for creating command-line tools. By leveraging Python's built-in modules and third-party libraries, you can develop robust and feature-rich command-line applications that can automate repetitive tasks, process data, and interact with various systems and services.

In this section, we will explore the process of creating a command-line tool in Python. We'll cover the fundamental concepts, learn how to parse command-line arguments, and develop a practical example that demonstrates the implementation of a simple command-line tool.

Understanding Command-Line Tools

Before diving into the code, let's first understand what command-line tools are and why they are essential in the world of software development.

A command-line tool, also known as a command-line interface (CLI) application, is a program that accepts input and executes commands through a text-based interface, typically a terminal or command prompt. These tools are often used by developers, system administrators, and power users who prefer a more efficient and scriptable way of interacting with applications and systems.

Command-line tools offer several advantages over graphical user interfaces (GUIs), including:

1. Automation: Command-line tools are highly scriptable, allowing for the automation of repetitive tasks and the creation of complex workflows.
2. Efficiency: With command-line tools, users can quickly execute commands and perform operations without navigating through multiple menus or windows.
3. Portability: Command-line tools are often platform-independent and can be used on various operating systems, making them highly portable and versatile.

4. Reproducibility: Command-line operations can be easily documented and shared, ensuring reproducibility and consistency across different environments.

Building a Command-Line Tool in Python

To create a command-line tool in Python, we'll leverage the `argparse` module, which is part of the Python standard library. This module provides a convenient way to handle command-line arguments and options, making it easier to create user-friendly and robust command-line interfaces.

Here's a step-by-step guide to building a simple command-line tool in Python:

1. Import the necessary modules:

```python
import argparse
```

2. Create an argument parser:

```python
parser = argparse.ArgumentParser(description="A simple command-line tool.")
```

The `ArgumentParser` class is the entry point for creating and configuring your command-line interface.

3. Define command-line arguments and options:

```python
parser.add_argument("input_file", help="Path to the input file.")
parser.add_argument("-o", "--output", help="Path to the output file.")
parser.add_argument("-v", "--verbose", action="store_true", help="Enable
verbose output.")
```

In this step, we use the `add_argument` method to define the expected command-line arguments and options. Each argument or option can have a name, a help message, and various configurations, such as whether it's required or optional, its data type, and more.

4. Parse the command-line arguments:

```python
args = parser.parse_args()
```

The `parse_args` method is used to parse the command-line arguments provided by the user and store them in the `args` object.

5. Implement the tool's functionality:

```python
def process_file(input_file, output_file, verbose):
    # Implement your tool's functionality here
    # Read data from the input file
    # Perform operations on the data
    # Write the output to the specified file or display it in the terminal

    if verbose:
        print("Processing completed successfully.")

if __name__ == "__main__":
    process_file(args.input_file, args.output, args.verbose)
```

In this step, you'll implement the core functionality of your command-line tool. This could involve reading data from an input file, performing operations or transformations on the data, and writing the output to a specified file or displaying it in the terminal.

The `process_file` function takes the parsed command-line arguments as input and executes the tool's logic accordingly.

6. Run the command-line tool:

To run your command-line tool, you can execute the Python script from the terminal or command prompt, passing the required arguments and options. For example:

```
python my_tool.py input.txt -o output.txt -v
```

This command will run the `my_tool.py` script, providing `input.txt` as the input file, `output.txt` as the output file, and enabling verbose output.

Best Practices for Creating Command-Line Tools

While creating command-line tools in Python, it's essential to follow best practices to ensure that your tools are user-friendly, maintainable, and efficient. Here are some guidelines to keep in mind:

1. Write clear and concise help messages: Provide clear and concise help messages for your command-line arguments and options. This will make it easier for users to understand how to use your tool effectively.

2. Handle errors gracefully: Implement robust error handling mechanisms to gracefully handle invalid input, file errors, or other exceptional situations. Display informative error messages to help users understand and resolve issues.

3. Provide default values and sensible defaults: When appropriate, provide default values for command-line arguments or options to simplify the user experience. Additionally, ensure that your default values are sensible and meaningful.

4. Consider cross-platform compatibility: If your command-line tool needs to run on multiple platforms (e.g., Windows, macOS, Linux), ensure that your code and dependencies are cross-platform compatible.

5. Implement logging and verbose output: Consider implementing logging mechanisms and verbose output options to provide users with additional information about the tool's execution and progress, especially for long-running or complex operations.

6. Write tests: As with any software development project, writing tests for your command-line tool is crucial for ensuring its correctness, reliability, and maintainability.

7. Document your tool: Provide clear and comprehensive documentation for your command-line tool, including installation instructions, usage examples, and descriptions of the available arguments and options.

8. Consider packaging and distribution: If your command-line tool is intended for wider distribution, consider packaging it as a Python package or distribution, making it easier for users to install and use your tool.

By following these best practices, you can create command-line tools in Python that are user-friendly, efficient, and maintainable, allowing you and others to automate tasks and streamline workflows effectively.

Developing a GUI Application

In the world of software development, graphical user interfaces (GUIs) have become an integral part of modern applications, providing users with a visually appealing and intuitive way to interact with programs. GUI applications offer a user-friendly experience by presenting information and controls in a graphical format, making it easier for users to navigate, input data, and perform various tasks.

Python, with its rich ecosystem of libraries and frameworks, offers powerful tools for building GUI applications. One of the most popular and cross-platform GUI toolkits for Python is Tkinter, which is included in the standard Python distribution. Additionally, there are third-party libraries like PyQt, wxPython, and Kivy, which provide more advanced features and functionalities for GUI development.

In this section, we will focus on developing a simple GUI application using Tkinter, a lightweight and cross-platform GUI toolkit. We'll explore the fundamental concepts, learn how to create and customize GUI elements, and develop a practical example that demonstrates the implementation of a basic GUI application.

Understanding GUI Applications

Before diving into the code, let's first understand what GUI applications are and why they are essential in the world of software development.

A GUI application is a program that provides a graphical interface for users to interact with, rather than relying solely on text-based interfaces or command-line tools. GUI applications typically consist of various graphical elements, such as windows, buttons, menus, text boxes, and other controls, which allow users to perform different actions and tasks.

GUI applications offer several advantages over command-line or text-based interfaces, including:

1. User-friendliness: GUI applications provide a more intuitive and visually appealing experience for users, making it easier for them to navigate and interact with the application.
2. Accessibility: By presenting information and controls in a graphical format, GUI applications can be more accessible to a wider range of users, including those with limited technical expertise.
3. Consistency: GUI frameworks and toolkits provide a consistent look and feel across different applications, making it easier for users to adapt to new software.
4. Interactivity: GUI applications allow for real-time user input and interaction, enabling dynamic updates and immediate feedback.

Building a GUI Application with Tkinter in Python

To create a GUI application in Python using Tkinter, we'll follow these steps:

1. Import the necessary modules:

```python
import tkinter as tk
```

2. Create the main window:

```python
root = tk.Tk()
```

The `Tk` class is the main entry point for creating a Tkinter application. It represents the main window of the GUI.

3. Add GUI elements:

```python
# Create a label
label = tk.Label(root, text="Hello, World!")
label.pack()

# Create a button
button = tk.Button(root, text="Click me!")
button.pack()
```

In this step, we create GUI elements such as labels and buttons using the corresponding Tkinter classes (`Label` and `Button`). These elements are added to the main window using the `pack` method, which automatically arranges the elements in the window.

4. Define event handlers:

```python
def button_clicked():
    print("Button clicked!")

button.config(command=button_clicked)
```

Event handlers are functions that are executed when specific events occur, such as a button click or a key press. In this example, we define a `button_clicked` function and associate it with the button's `command` option using the `config` method.

5. Run the main event loop:

```python
root.mainloop()
```

The `mainloop` method starts the main event loop, which continuously listens for and responds to user events, such as mouse clicks or keyboard inputs. This keeps the GUI application running and interactive.

6. Optional: Add more GUI elements and functionality:

Depending on your application's requirements, you can add more GUI elements, such as text boxes, menus, and canvas objects, and implement additional functionality, such as data processing, file operations, or network communication.

Best Practices for GUI Development in Python

While developing GUI applications in Python, it's essential to follow best practices to ensure that your applications are user-friendly, maintainable, and efficient. Here are some guidelines to keep in mind:

1. Separate concerns: Separate the GUI logic from the application logic to promote modular and maintainable code. This can be achieved by using design patterns like Model-View-Controller (MVC) or Model-View-Presenter (MVP).

2. Follow platform-specific guidelines: Adhere to the design guidelines and conventions of the target platform (e.g., Windows, macOS, or Linux) to provide a consistent and familiar user experience.

3. Implement responsive and resizable layouts: Design your GUI layouts to be responsive and resizable, ensuring that elements adapt properly to different window sizes and screen resolutions.

4. Handle user input and validation: Implement proper input validation and error handling to ensure that your application can gracefully handle invalid or unexpected user input.

5. Provide feedback and progress indicators: Keep users informed about long-running operations or processes by providing feedback and progress indicators, such as progress bars or status messages.

6. Consider accessibility: Design your GUI with accessibility in mind, ensuring that it can be used by users with disabilities, such as those who rely on screen readers or alternative input methods.

7. Write tests: As with any software development project, writing tests for your GUI application is crucial for ensuring its correctness, reliability, and maintainability.

8. Document your code: Provide clear and comprehensive documentation for your GUI application, including descriptions of the application's functionality, usage instructions, and explanations of the code structure and components.

9. Consider packaging and distribution: If your GUI application is intended for wider distribution, consider packaging it as a standalone executable or installer to make it easier for users to install and run your application.

By following these best practices, you can create user-friendly, maintainable, and efficient GUI applications in Python that provide a seamless and enjoyable experience for your users.

Working with APIs and Data Analysis

In today's data-driven world, the ability to access and analyze data from various sources has become increasingly important. With the proliferation of web services and online platforms, accessing and working with data through Application Programming Interfaces (APIs) has become a crucial skill for developers and data professionals alike. Combining API data with the power of Python's data analysis capabilities opens up a world of possibilities for gaining insights, making informed decisions, and building data-driven applications.

This section will introduce you to the fundamentals of working with APIs and performing data analysis in Python. We'll cover the basics of APIs, explore Python libraries for making API requests and handling data, and dive into practical examples of data analysis tasks. By the end of this guide, you'll have a solid understanding of how to retrieve data from APIs and leverage Python's powerful data analysis tools to extract meaningful insights from that data.

An Application Programming Interface (API) is a set of rules and protocols that defines how different software components should interact with each other. APIs act as intermediaries, enabling different applications or systems to communicate and exchange data in a standardized and controlled manner.

APIs are widely used in various domains, including web development, mobile applications, and data integration. They provide a structured way to access and manipulate data from external sources, such as social media platforms, weather services, financial institutions, and more.

APIs typically follow a client-server architecture, where the client (your application or script) sends a request to the server (the API provider), and the server responds with the requested data or performs the requested action.

Working with APIs in Python

Python provides several libraries and modules for interacting with APIs, making it a powerful language for working with online data sources. Two popular libraries for making API requests in Python are the built-in `urllib` module and the third-party `requests` library.

The `urllib` module is part of Python's standard library and provides a low-level interface for making HTTP requests. While it is a powerful tool, its syntax can be somewhat complex for beginners.

The `requests` library, on the other hand, offers a more user-friendly and intuitive interface for making HTTP requests. It simplifies the process of sending HTTP/1.1 requests, handling responses, and working with various data formats like JSON and XML.

Here's an example of how to use the `requests` library to make a simple GET request to an API:

```python
import requests

# Send a GET request to the API
response = requests.get("https://api.example.com/data")

# Check if the request was successful
if response.status_code == 200:
    # Get the data from the response
    data = response.json()
    # Process the data as needed
    print(data)
else:
    print(f"Error: {response.status_code}")
```

In this example, we import the `requests` library and use the `get` function to send a GET request to the specified API endpoint. The `response` object contains the server's response, including the status code and the data payload. We check if the request was successful (status code 200) and then access the response data using the `json` method.

Working with Data in Python

Once you've retrieved data from an API, you'll often need to perform various data analysis and manipulation tasks. Python provides a rich ecosystem of libraries and tools for working with structured and unstructured data, making it an excellent choice for data analysis and processing.

Two popular libraries for data analysis in Python are Pandas and NumPy. Pandas is a powerful data manipulation and analysis library that provides high-performance, easy-to-use data structures and data analysis tools. NumPy, on the other hand, is a fundamental library for scientific computing in Python, providing support for large, multi-dimensional arrays and matrices, along with a collection of high-level mathematical functions to operate on these arrays.

Here's an example of how to use Pandas to read and analyze data from a CSV file:

```python
import pandas as pd

# Read data from a CSV file
data = pd.read_csv("data.csv")

# Display the first few rows of the data
print(data.head())

# Get information about the data
print(data.info())

# Calculate summary statistics
print(data.describe())

# Filter data based on a condition
filtered_data = data[data["age"] > 30]
print(filtered_data)
```

In this example, we import the Pandas library and use the `read_csv` function to read data from a CSV file. We then use various Pandas functions to explore and analyze the data, such as `head` to display the first few rows, `info` to get information about the data structure and data types, `describe` to calculate summary statistics, and boolean indexing to filter the data based on a condition.

Data Visualization in Python

Data visualization is an essential aspect of data analysis, as it helps to communicate insights and patterns in a clear and intuitive manner. Python provides several powerful data visualization libraries, such as Matplotlib, Seaborn, and Plotly, which allow you to create a wide range of static and interactive visualizations.

Matplotlib is a low-level plotting library that provides a MATLAB-like interface for creating 2D and 3D plots, histograms, bar charts, scatter plots, and more. Seaborn is a higher-level data visualization library built on top of Matplotlib, providing a more intuitive and attractive interface for creating statistical graphics.

Here's an example of how to use Matplotlib and Seaborn to create a simple line plot and a scatter plot with a regression line:

```python
import matplotlib.pyplot as plt
```

```python
import seaborn as sns
import pandas as pd

# Load data from a CSV file
data = pd.read_csv("data.csv")

# Create a line plot using Matplotlib
plt.figure(figsize=(8, 6))
plt.plot(data["year"], data["population"])
plt.xlabel("Year")
plt.ylabel("Population")
plt.title("Population Growth Over Time")
plt.show()

# Create a scatter plot with a regression line using Seaborn
sns.regplot(x="age", y="income", data=data)
plt.title("Income vs. Age")
plt.show()
```

In this example, we import the necessary libraries (`matplotlib.pyplot`, `seaborn`, and `pandas`), load data from a CSV file, and create two visualizations: a line plot showing population growth over time using Matplotlib, and a scatter plot with a regression line showing the relationship between age and income using Seaborn.

Best Practices for Working with APIs and Data Analysis

While working with APIs and performing data analysis in Python, it's essential to follow best practices to ensure efficient, maintainable, and reproducible code. Here are some guidelines to keep in mind:

1. Modular and reusable code: Write modular and reusable code by separating concerns and organizing your code into functions and modules. This will make your code easier to maintain, test, and extend.

2. Error handling and input validation: Implement proper error handling and input validation to ensure that your code can gracefully handle exceptions, invalid data, and unexpected situations.

3. Documentation and comments: Document your code with clear and concise comments, docstrings, and external documentation (e.g., README files). This will make it easier for others (and your future self) to understand and maintain your code.

4. Version control and collaboration: Use version control systems like Git to track changes to your code, collaborate with others, and manage different versions and branches of your project.

5. Testing and quality assurance: Write unit tests and integration tests to ensure the correctness and reliability of your code, especially when working with external APIs or processing critical data.

6. Performance optimization: Consider performance implications when working with large datasets or making numerous API requests. Implement techniques like caching, parallelization, and optimized data structures to improve the efficiency of your code.

7. Data privacy and security: When working with sensitive or personal data, ensure that you follow best practices for data privacy and security, such as anonymizing or encrypting data, adhering to data protection regulations, and implementing access controls.

8. Reproducibility and collaboration: When working on data analysis projects, ensure that your code and analysis are reproducible by others. Share your code, data, and documentation, and consider using tools like Jupyter Notebooks or literate programming techniques to facilitate collaboration and reproducibility.

9. Continuous learning and staying up-to-date: The Python ecosystem and data analysis landscape are constantly evolving, with new libraries, tools, and techniques emerging regularly. Stay up-to-date by following industry news, attending conferences or online workshops, and continuously learning and improving your skills.

By following these best practices, you can create efficient, maintainable, and reproducible code for working with APIs and performing data analysis in Python, enabling you to extract valuable insights and build robust, data-driven applications.

Advanced Topics and Resources

While this section provides a solid foundation for working with APIs and data analysis in Python, there are many advanced topics and resources available for those seeking to deepen their knowledge and skills:

1. Web scraping and parsing: Beyond APIs, you can also extract data from websites using web scraping techniques and libraries like Beautiful Soup and Scrapy.

2. Natural Language Processing (NLP): If you're working with text data, you may want to explore NLP libraries like NLTK and spaCy for tasks such as text preprocessing, sentiment analysis, and topic modeling.

3. Machine Learning and Deep Learning: Python's rich ecosystem of libraries like scikit-learn, TensorFlow, and PyTorch make it a popular choice for implementing machine learning and deep learning models for tasks like classification, regression, and predictive modeling.

4. Big Data and Distributed Computing: For working with large-scale data, you may want to explore tools and frameworks like Apache Spark, Dask, and Ray for distributed computing and parallel processing.

5. Data Engineering and ETL: If you're dealing with complex data pipelines and ETL (Extract, Transform, Load) processes, consider learning about libraries and frameworks like Apache Airflow, Luigi, and Prefect.

6. Data Visualization and Dashboards: For advanced data visualization and interactive dashboards, explore libraries like Plotly, Bokeh, and Dash, as well as business intelligence tools like Power BI and Tableau.

7. Cloud Computing and APIs: As more and more data and services move to the cloud, it's essential to learn about cloud computing platforms like AWS, Google Cloud, and Microsoft Azure, and how to interact with their APIs and services using Python.

8. Online courses and tutorials: Platforms like Coursera, Udemy, and DataCamp offer a wide range of online courses and tutorials on topics related to Python, data analysis, machine learning, and more, taught by industry experts and top-tier instructors.

9. Books and documentation: Continuously refer to authoritative books, documentation, and online resources to deepen your understanding of Python, data analysis techniques, and related libraries and tools.

10. Community and networking: Participate in online communities, forums, and local meetups to connect with other Python and data professionals, share knowledge, and stay up-to-date with the latest trends and best practices.

By exploring these advanced topics and resources, you can continue to expand your skills and knowledge in working with APIs and data analysis in Python, enabling you to tackle increasingly complex and challenging projects in the field of data science and application development.

Chapter 9: Python Ecosystem and Resources

Popular Python Libraries and Frameworks

Python is a versatile and powerful programming language that has gained widespread popularity across various domains, including web development, data analysis, scientific computing, machine learning, and more. One of the key strengths of Python lies in its extensive ecosystem of libraries and frameworks, which provide a vast array of functionalities and tools to streamline development and enhance productivity.

In this chapter, we'll explore some of the most popular Python libraries and frameworks, understanding their purposes, key features, and use cases. Whether you're a novice programmer or an experienced developer looking to expand your Python knowledge, this guide will provide you with a solid foundation to navigate the rich Python ecosystem.

1. NumPy: The Foundation for Scientific Computing

NumPy (Numerical Python) is a fundamental library for scientific computing in Python. It provides support for large, multi-dimensional arrays and matrices, along with a collection of high-level mathematical functions to operate on these arrays. NumPy serves as the backbone for many other scientific and numerical libraries in the Python ecosystem.

Key features:
- Efficient storage and manipulation of large numerical arrays and matrices
- Extensive mathematical functions for operations like linear algebra, Fourier analysis, and random number generation
- Broadcasting capabilities for performing operations on arrays with different shapes
- Integration with other libraries like SciPy, Pandas, and Matplotlib

Use cases:
- Linear algebra and matrix operations
- Signal and image processing
- Statistical analysis
- Scientific simulations and modeling

2. Pandas: Data Analysis Made Simple

Pandas is a powerful data manipulation and analysis library that provides high-performance, easy-to-use data structures and data analysis tools. It is particularly well-suited for working with structured (tabular) data, making it an essential tool for data scientists, analysts, and researchers.

Key features:
- Two main data structures: Series (1D) and DataFrame (2D)
- Efficient handling of missing data and data alignment
- Powerful data indexing and selection capabilities

- Data cleaning, merging, reshaping, and filtering operations
- Reading and writing data from various file formats (CSV, Excel, SQL databases, etc.)
- Data visualization with integration to Matplotlib

Use cases:
- Data wrangling and cleaning
- Exploratory data analysis
- Statistical analysis and modeling
- Time series analysis
- Data preprocessing for machine learning

3. Matplotlib: Visualizing Data with Clarity

Matplotlib is a comprehensive library for creating static, animated, and interactive visualizations in Python. It provides a wide range of plotting utilities for creating 2D and 3D plots, histograms, bar charts, scatter plots, and more. Matplotlib serves as the foundation for many other visualization libraries in the Python ecosystem.

Key features:
- Low-level plotting functions for creating various types of plots
- Support for different output formats (PNG, PDF, SVG, etc.)
- Customizable plot styles, colors, and layouts
- Integration with other libraries like NumPy, Pandas, and SciPy
- Interactive plotting with backends like Qt and Tkinter

Use cases:
- Data visualization and exploration
- Scientific and engineering plotting
- Publication-quality figure generation
- Interactive data visualization applications

4. Scikit-learn: Machine Learning Made Accessible

Scikit-learn is a powerful and user-friendly machine learning library for Python. It provides a consistent and streamlined interface for various machine learning algorithms, making it easy to build and evaluate predictive models. Scikit-learn is widely used in academia and industry for a wide range of applications.

Key features:
- Implementations of a wide range of machine learning algorithms (classification, regression, clustering, dimensionality reduction, etc.)
- Data preprocessing and feature engineering utilities
- Model evaluation and model selection tools
- Efficient handling of large datasets
- Compatibility with other scientific libraries like NumPy and Pandas

Use cases:
- Supervised learning tasks (classification and regression)

- Unsupervised learning tasks (clustering and dimensionality reduction)
- Model selection and evaluation
- Data preprocessing and feature engineering
- Machine learning pipelines and workflows

5. Django: The Web Framework for Perfectionists

Django is a high-level Python web framework that follows the Model-View-Template (MVT) architectural pattern. It emphasizes reusability, rapid development, and adherence to the "Don't Repeat Yourself" (DRY) principle, making it an excellent choice for building robust and scalable web applications.

Key features:
- Built-in support for common web development tasks (URL routing, database integration, form handling, user authentication, etc.)
- Powerful Object-Relational Mapping (ORM) for interacting with databases
- Admin interface for managing application data
- Robust security features
- Internationalization and localization support
- Extensive third-party package ecosystem

Use cases:
- Building web applications and APIs
- Content management systems
- E-commerce platforms
- Social networking sites
- Data-driven web applications

6. Flask: The Microframework for Python Web Development

Flask is a lightweight and flexible Python web framework that follows the microservices architecture. It is designed to be easy to learn and get started with, while still providing the essential tools and features needed for building web applications and APIs.

Key features:
- Minimalistic and modular design
- Built-in development server and debugger
- Support for routing, request handling, and templates
- Extension ecosystem for adding functionality (e.g., databases, authentication, caching)
- WSGI compliant and compatible with various web servers

Use cases:
- Building small to medium-sized web applications and APIs
- Prototyping and experimentation
- Microservices and RESTful APIs
- Personal projects and hobby websites

7. TensorFlow and PyTorch: The Powerhouses of Deep Learning

TensorFlow and PyTorch are two of the most popular deep learning frameworks in the Python ecosystem. While they have different philosophies and approaches, both provide powerful tools and APIs for building and training complex neural networks and machine learning models.

TensorFlow:
- Developed by Google
- Focuses on computational graphs and symbolic programming
- Supports distributed training and deployment
- Extensive ecosystem of tools and libraries (Keras, TensorFlow Hub, TensorFlow Serving, etc.)

PyTorch:
- Developed by Facebook's AI Research lab
- Emphasizes dynamic computation graphs and imperative programming style
- Efficient GPU acceleration and support for parallel computing
- Strong community support and active development

Use cases:
- Building and training deep neural networks
- Computer vision tasks (image classification, object detection, etc.)
- Natural language processing tasks (text classification, machine translation, etc.)
- Generative models and unsupervised learning
- Reinforcement learning and robotics

8. Beautiful Soup: Web Scraping Made Easy

Beautiful Soup is a Python library designed for web scraping purposes. It provides a simple and intuitive way to parse HTML and XML documents, making it easier to extract and manipulate data from websites.

Key features:
- Robust parsing of malformed or non-standard HTML/XML documents
- Navigating and searching the parsed tree using various methods and filters
- Modifying and transforming the parsed data
- Integration with other libraries like requests for fetching web content

Use cases:
- Web scraping and data extraction
- Web content mining and analysis
- Automated testing and monitoring of web applications
- Building web crawlers and scrapers

9. SQLAlchemy: The Python SQL Toolkit and Object-Relational Mapper

SQLAlchemy is a Python SQL toolkit and Object-Relational Mapping (ORM) library that provides a set of high-level APIs for interacting with databases. It abstracts the underlying database engine, allowing you to write database-agnostic code and easily switch between different database systems.

Key features:
- Database-agnostic ORM for mapping Python objects to database tables
- SQL query construction and execution
- Support for various database systems (SQLite, PostgreSQL, MySQL, Oracle, etc.)
- Database migration and versioning tools
- Integration with other Python web frameworks like Flask and Django

Use cases:
- Building database-driven applications
- Object-relational mapping and data modeling
- Database migration and schema management
- Querying and manipulating data in various database systems

10. Requests: The Human Side of HTTP in Python

Requests is a popular Python library for making HTTP requests and interacting with web services and APIs. It provides a simple and intuitive interface for sending HTTP/1.1 requests, handling responses, and working with various data formats like JSON and XML.

Key features:
- Simple and user-friendly API for making HTTP requests (GET, POST, PUT, DELETE, etc.)
- Handling of cookies, headers, and other request/response data
- Support for file uploads and streaming data
- Exception handling and error reporting
- Integration with other libraries like Beautiful Soup for web scraping

Use cases:
- Interacting with web services and APIs
- Web scraping and data extraction
- Automating HTTP-based tasks and workflows
- Building API clients and wrappers

These are just a few examples of the many powerful libraries and frameworks available in the Python ecosystem. As you continue your journey in Python programming, you'll discover numerous other tools and libraries tailored to specific domains and use cases, such as data visualization (Seaborn, Plotly), natural language processing (NLTK, spaCy), computer vision (OpenCV), and more.

When choosing which libraries and frameworks to learn and use, it's important to consider your specific project requirements, development goals, and the trade-offs between simplicity and complexity. Some libraries are designed to be lightweight and focused, while others offer comprehensive and feature-rich solutions.

Additionally, it's crucial to stay up-to-date with the latest developments in the Python ecosystem, as new libraries and tools are constantly emerging, and existing ones are continually being updated with new features and improvements. Engaging with the Python community, attending conferences and meetups, and following reputable online resources can help you stay informed about the latest trends and best practices.

Python Package Management

In the world of software development, managing dependencies and third-party packages is a crucial aspect of working with any programming language or framework. Python, with its vast and ever-growing ecosystem of libraries and tools, is no exception. Effective package management ensures that your Python projects have access to the required dependencies, enabling seamless installation, updating, and removal of packages.

This section to Python package management will introduce you to the fundamental concepts and tools used for managing Python packages. We'll explore the Python packaging ecosystem, learn about popular package managers like pip and conda, and dive into best practices for managing dependencies in your projects. By the end of this guide, you'll have a solid understanding of how to effectively manage Python packages, ensuring that your projects remain organized, maintainable, and up-to-date.

Understanding the Python Packaging Ecosystem

Before diving into the specifics of package management, it's essential to understand the Python packaging ecosystem and its key components:

1. **Python Packages:** A Python package is a collection of modules that can be distributed and installed as a single unit. Packages can contain Python code, data files, documentation, and other resources. They provide a way to organize and share reusable code across different projects.

2. **Python Package Index (PyPI):** PyPI is the official repository for Python packages. It's a centralized location where developers can upload and share their packages, making them available for others to discover and install. PyPI hosts thousands of packages for a wide range of applications and domains.

3. **Package Managers:** Package managers are tools that automate the process of installing, upgrading, and removing packages. They handle dependencies, version management, and ensure that packages are installed correctly and consistently across different systems.

4. **Virtual Environments:** Virtual environments are isolated Python environments that allow you to manage dependencies and packages on a per-project basis. This means that you can have different versions of packages installed in different virtual environments, preventing conflicts and ensuring consistent behavior across projects.

5. **Dependency Management:** Dependency management is the process of tracking and managing the external packages that your project relies on, ensuring that they are compatible and up-to-date. This is typically done using package managers and configuration files like `requirements.txt`.

Popular Python Package Managers

Python has several package managers available, each with its own strengths and use cases. In this guide, we'll focus on the two most widely used package managers: pip and conda.

1. pip: The Python Package Installer

pip is the official package installer for Python and is included by default with Python installations. It's a command-line tool that allows you to install, upgrade, and remove Python packages from the Python Package Index (PyPI) or other package repositories.

Here are some common pip commands:

- `pip install package_name`: Install a package
- `pip install -r requirements.txt`: Install packages from a requirements file
- `pip uninstall package_name`: Uninstall a package
- `pip list`: List installed packages
- `pip freeze > requirements.txt`: Save installed packages to a requirements file

Example: Installing the `requests` package using pip:

```
pip install requests
```

2. conda: The Cross-Platform Package Manager

conda is a cross-platform package manager and environment management system developed by Anaconda, Inc. It is particularly popular in the data science and scientific computing communities due to its support for managing packages across multiple languages (Python, R, Julia, etc.) and its ability to create isolated environments with specific package versions.

Here are some common conda commands:

- `conda create --name myenv python=3.9`: Create a new environment named "myenv" with Python 3.9
- `conda activate myenv`: Activate the "myenv" environment
- `conda install package_name`: Install a package in the active environment
- `conda remove package_name`: Remove a package from the active environment
- `conda list`: List installed packages in the active environment
- `conda env export > environment.yml`: Export the active environment to a YAML file

Example: Creating a new conda environment and installing NumPy:

```
conda create --name myenv python=3.9
conda activate myenv
conda install numpy
```

Managing Dependencies and Virtual Environments

Effective dependency management is crucial for ensuring that your Python projects run consistently across different environments and systems. It also helps to maintain a clean and organized codebase by separating project dependencies from system-level packages.

1. Virtual Environments

Virtual environments are isolated Python environments that allow you to manage dependencies and packages on a per-project basis. By creating a virtual environment for each project, you can ensure that the project's dependencies are isolated from other projects and the system's Python installation.

Python includes the `venv` module for creating and managing virtual environments. Here's an example of how to create and activate a virtual environment:

```
# Create a new virtual environment
python -m venv myenv

# Activate the virtual environment
# On Windows
myenv\Scripts\activate

# On Unix/macOS
source myenv/bin/activate
```

Once a virtual environment is activated, any packages you install will be isolated within that environment, preventing conflicts with other projects or the system's Python installation.

2. Requirements Files

Requirements files are text files that list the dependencies required by your Python project. These files are typically named `requirements.txt` and can be used with package managers like pip and conda to install the required packages in a consistent and reproducible manner.

Here's an example of a `requirements.txt` file:

```
numpy==1.21.5
pandas==1.3.5
scikit-learn==1.0.2
```

To install the packages listed in the `requirements.txt` file, you can use the following command with pip:

```
pip install -r requirements.txt
```

Similarly, conda supports environment files in the YAML format (e.g., `environment.yml`), which can be used to create and manage conda environments with specific package versions and dependencies.

3. Environment Management Tools

While virtual environments and requirements files provide a solid foundation for dependency management, there are additional tools and frameworks available to streamline the process further. Two popular tools are Poetry and Pipenv.

Poetry is a modern dependency management tool for Python that focuses on simplicity, reproducibility, and ease of use. It combines the functionality of package management, virtual environment management, and build system into a single tool.

Pipenv is another dependency management tool that aims to bring the best of all packaging worlds (bundler, composer, npm, cargo, yarn, etc.) to the Python world. It automatically creates and manages virtual environments and allows you to easily install, update, and remove packages.

These tools provide additional features and capabilities for managing dependencies, such as locking package versions, resolving dependency conflicts, and generating dependency graphs.

Best Practices for Python Package Management

Effective package management involves following a set of best practices to ensure that your projects remain organized, maintainable, and consistent across different environments. Here are some recommended best practices:

1. Use Virtual Environments: Always use virtual environments for your Python projects. This will prevent conflicts between project dependencies and system-level packages, ensuring a clean and reproducible environment for your project.

2. Maintain Requirements Files: Keep your project dependencies documented in a requirements file (`requirements.txt` or `environment.yml`). This makes it easy to install and share the required packages with others, ensuring consistent behavior across different environments.

3. Pin Package Versions: When specifying package dependencies in your requirements files, it's generally recommended to pin the package versions to specific releases. This prevents unexpected behavior caused by updates to dependencies and ensures reproducible builds.

4. Separate Development and Production Dependencies: Consider separating development dependencies (e.g., testing frameworks, linters, debugging tools) from production dependencies. This can be achieved by having separate requirements files or using tools like Poetry or Pipenv, which support different dependency groups.

5. Regularly Update Dependencies: Periodically review and update your project dependencies to ensure that you're using the latest stable versions and to address any potential security vulnerabilities or bug fixes.

6. Use Trusted Package Sources: Install packages from trusted and reputable sources, such as the Python Package Index (PyPI) or the Anaconda Cloud repository. Be cautious when installing packages from untrusted or unofficial sources, as they may introduce security risks or compatibility issues.

7. Document Dependency Management Processes: Clearly document your dependency management processes, including how to set up virtual environments, install dependencies, and update packages. This will help ensure a smooth onboarding process for new team members and facilitate collaboration.

8. Consider Using Environment Management Tools: Evaluate the use of environment management tools like Poetry or Pipenv, especially for larger or more complex projects. These tools can simplify the dependency management process and provide additional features and capabilities.

9. Automate Dependency Management: Integrate dependency management tasks into your project's build and deployment processes. This can include automating the creation and activation of virtual environments, installing dependencies from requirements files, and checking for outdated or vulnerable packages.

10. Collaborate and Share Knowledge: Engage with the Python community, attend meetups and conferences, and stay up-to-date with the latest best practices and tools for package management. Sharing knowledge and experiences can help improve your team's dependency management practices.

Advanced Topics and Additional Resources

While this section provides a solid foundation for Python package management, there are several advanced topics and additional resources that you may find useful as you progress in your Python journey:

1. Python Packaging and Distribution: Learn about packaging your own Python projects for distribution on PyPI or other package repositories. This involves creating distributable packages, writing documentation, and following best practices for versioning and release management.

2. Continuous Integration and Deployment: Integrate your package management processes with continuous integration and deployment (CI/CD) pipelines. This ensures that your projects are consistently built, tested, and deployed with the correct dependencies and package versions.

3. Containerization and Reproducible Environments: Explore containerization tools like Docker and container management platforms like Kubernetes. These tools can help ensure consistent and reproducible environments for your Python applications, including dependencies and system-level configurations.

4. Monorepos and Workspace Management: For larger projects or organizations, consider adopting monorepo architectures and workspace management tools like Pants or Bazel. These tools can help manage dependencies and build processes across multiple Python projects or codebases.

5. Advanced Dependency Management Tools: Investigate more advanced dependency management tools and frameworks, such as Poetry, Pipenv, Pip-tools, and Conda-forge. These tools offer additional features and capabilities for managing dependencies, resolving conflicts, and optimizing package installations.

6. Security and Vulnerability Management: Learn about tools and practices for managing security vulnerabilities in Python packages, such as safety, bandit, and the Python Package Index's vulnerability advisories.

7. Python Packaging User Guide: Refer to the official Python Packaging User Guide (https://packaging.python.org/) for comprehensive documentation and guidelines on packaging, distributing, and managing Python packages.

8. Python Packaging Authority (PyPA): Follow the work of the Python Packaging Authority (PyPA), the group responsible for maintaining and improving the Python packaging ecosystem, including tools like pip, setuptools, and PyPI.

9. Online Courses and Tutorials: Explore online courses and tutorials on Python package management and packaging from reputable sources like Coursera, Udemy, and Real Python.

10. Community Resources: Engage with the Python community through forums, mailing lists, and online communities like the Python Packaging Discourse (https://packaging.python.org/en/latest/discussions.html) to stay updated on the latest trends, best practices, and discussions related to Python package management.

Python Documentation and Community

As a beginner in the world of Python programming, you'll quickly discover that the language's documentation and community resources are invaluable assets in your learning journey. Python boasts an extensive and well-maintained documentation ecosystem, as well as a vibrant and supportive community of developers, enthusiasts, and professionals.

This guide aims to introduce you to the various documentation resources available for Python, as well as the diverse and inclusive community that surrounds this popular programming language. By leveraging these resources effectively, you'll not only enhance your understanding of Python but also gain access to a wealth of knowledge, support, and collaboration opportunities.

Python Documentation Resources

Documentation plays a crucial role in learning and mastering any programming language, and Python is no exception. The Python ecosystem offers a comprehensive suite of documentation resources designed to cater to users of all skill levels, from absolute beginners to experienced developers.

1. The Python Documentation

The official Python documentation, hosted at https://docs.python.org, is a comprehensive and authoritative source of information for the Python language and its standard library. This documentation is meticulously maintained by the Python Software Foundation and is updated with each new release of Python.

The Python documentation is divided into several sections, including:

- Tutorial: An excellent starting point for beginners, providing a gentle introduction to Python's syntax, data types, and programming concepts.
- Library Reference: A comprehensive reference guide for Python's extensive standard library, covering all built-in modules and functions.
- Language Reference: A detailed description of Python's syntax and core language features, including data types, expressions, and statements.
- Installing Python: Instructions and guidance for installing Python on various platforms and operating systems.
- How-to Guides: Practical guides covering a wide range of topics, such as writing command-line tools, working with files and directories, and more.
- Python FAQs: A collection of frequently asked questions and their corresponding answers, addressing common queries and misconceptions.

The Python documentation is available in multiple formats, including HTML, PDF, and plain text, making it accessible across various devices and platforms.

2. Python Enhancement Proposals (PEPs)

Python Enhancement Proposals (PEPs) are design documents that describe proposed changes, enhancements, or new features for the Python language and its ecosystem. PEPs serve as a collaborative platform for the Python community to discuss, review, and ultimately accept or reject proposed changes.

PEPs cover a wide range of topics, including language features, standard library additions, coding style guidelines, and more. They provide valuable insights into the rationale behind design decisions and offer a glimpse into the future direction of Python.

The official PEP index (https://www.python.org/dev/peps/) is a comprehensive collection of all accepted and proposed PEPs, allowing you to stay up-to-date with the latest developments and proposals in the Python community.

3. Third-Party Documentation and Resources

In addition to the official Python documentation, a vast ecosystem of third-party resources exists, ranging from tutorials and guides to reference materials and code samples. These resources are often created and maintained by Python enthusiasts, developers, and organizations, and can be invaluable for learning specific Python libraries, frameworks, or domain-specific applications.

Some popular third-party documentation resources include:

- Real Python (https://realpython.com): A comprehensive learning platform offering tutorials, articles, and video courses for Python developers of all skill levels.
- Python Documentation (https://devdocs.io/python~3.11/): A comprehensive offline Python documentation viewer, featuring the official Python documentation and select third-party libraries.

- Python Guides (https://pythonguides.com): A collection of tutorials, how-to guides, and code examples covering a wide range of Python topics and libraries.
- Python for You and Me (https://pymbook.readthedocs.io/): An introductory book on Python, designed for beginners and self-learners.

These third-party resources often complement the official Python documentation by providing alternative perspectives, practical examples, and in-depth explanations tailored to specific use cases or learning styles.

The Python Community

One of the greatest strengths of the Python programming language is its vibrant and welcoming community. The Python community is a diverse and inclusive group of individuals, ranging from beginners to experienced developers, educators, researchers, and professionals from various industries and backgrounds.

1. Online Communities and Forums

Online communities and forums are essential platforms for Python enthusiasts to connect, collaborate, and seek support. These online spaces foster knowledge sharing, provide opportunities for networking, and serve as valuable resources for asking questions and finding solutions to common challenges.

Some popular online communities and forums for Python include:

- Python Subreddit (https://www.reddit.com/r/Python/): A highly active and engaging community on Reddit, where Python enthusiasts share news, ask questions, and discuss various Python-related topics.
- Python Discord Server (https://discord.gg/python): A Discord server dedicated to Python, offering channels for discussions, coding help, and community events.
- Python Mailing Lists (https://mail.python.org/mailman/listinfo): A collection of mailing lists focused on various aspects of Python, including development, announcements, and specialized topics.
- Stack Overflow (https://stackoverflow.com/questions/tagged/python): A popular question and answer site where developers can ask and answer Python-related questions, as well as find solutions to common programming problems.

These online communities provide invaluable support and mentorship for beginners, while also fostering collaboration and knowledge sharing among experienced Python developers.

2. Local User Groups and Meetups

In addition to online communities, many cities and regions have local Python user groups and meetups that bring together Python enthusiasts for in-person events, talks, workshops, and networking opportunities.

Attending local Python meetups can be an excellent way to connect with fellow Python developers in your area, learn from experienced professionals, and stay up-to-date with the latest trends and best practices in the Python ecosystem.

To find local Python user groups and meetups in your area, you can search platforms like Meetup.com or Python.org's official user group directory (https://www.python.org/community/ug/).

3. Conferences and Events

Python conferences and events provide excellent opportunities for learning, networking, and staying ahead of the curve in the ever-evolving Python ecosystem. These events offer a diverse range of talks, workshops, and tutorials delivered by industry experts, core developers, and thought leaders in the Python community.

Some notable Python conferences and events include:

- PyCon (https://us.pycon.org/): The largest annual gathering of Python enthusiasts, featuring multiple tracks, tutorials, and opportunities for networking and collaboration.
- EuroPython (https://ep2023.europython.eu/): The largest European conference dedicated to the Python programming language, attracting attendees from around the world.
- PyCon India (https://in.pycon.org/): A regional Python conference held annually in India, offering a platform for the local and international Python community to connect and share knowledge.
- PyData (https://pydata.org/): A conference series focused on data science, machine learning, and data visualization using Python and its related ecosystem of tools and libraries.

Attending these conferences not only provides valuable learning opportunities but also allows you to connect with like-minded individuals, explore potential job opportunities, and contribute to the Python community.

4. Open-Source Contributions

The Python community is built on the principles of open-source collaboration and sharing. Contributing to open-source Python projects is not only a great way to give back to the community but also an excellent opportunity to learn, gain practical experience, and collaborate with experienced developers from around the world.

The Python Package Index (PyPI) (https://pypi.org/) is the official repository for open-source Python packages and libraries. Here, you can explore and contribute to a vast array of projects, ranging from small utility libraries to large-scale frameworks and applications.

Contributing to open-source Python projects can take many forms, including:

- Reporting and fixing bugs
- Implementing new features or enhancements
- Writing documentation and examples
- Translating documentation or code into different languages
- Participating in code reviews and discussions
- Testing and providing feedback on new releases

By actively contributing to open-source Python projects, you not only help to improve and shape the Python ecosystem but also gain valuable experience, build your portfolio, and establish yourself as a respected member of the Python community.

Best Practices for Engaging with the Python Community

Engaging with the Python community can be a rewarding and enriching experience, but it's important to follow best practices to ensure a positive and productive experience for all involved.

1. Be respectful and inclusive: The Python community values diversity and inclusivity. Treat all members with respect, regardless of their background, experience level, or opinions.

2. Follow community guidelines: Many online communities and open-source projects have established codes of conduct or guidelines. Familiarize yourself with these guidelines and follow them to maintain a positive and welcoming environment.

3. Ask good questions: When seeking help or guidance, be sure to provide clear and concise information about your problem, including any relevant code snippets, error messages, and steps you've taken to troubleshoot the issue. This will help others better understand and assist you.

4. Be patient and courteous: Remember that many community members contribute their time and expertise voluntarily. Be patient and courteous when seeking assistance or feedback.

5. Give back to the community: Consider giving back to the Python community by contributing to open-source projects, answering questions, or sharing your knowledge and experiences through blog posts, tutorials, or presentations.

6. Stay up-to-date: Keep an eye on community announcements, updates, and discussions to stay informed about the latest developments, trends, and best practices in the Python ecosystem.

7. Attend local events and conferences: Participate in local Python meetups and conferences to connect with other community members, learn from experts, and build your professional network.

8. Promote diversity and inclusion: Support and promote initiatives that foster diversity and inclusion within the Python community, ensuring that all voices and perspectives are heard and valued.

9. Respect intellectual property and licensing: When using or contributing to open-source Python projects, be mindful of intellectual property rights and follow the project's licensing terms and conditions.

10. Have fun and enjoy the journey: Above all, remember to have fun and enjoy the learning process. The Python community is a supportive and welcoming environment for individuals of all skill levels and backgrounds.

Where to Go from Here

Congratulations on embarking on your journey into the world of Python programming! By taking the time to learn the fundamentals of this versatile and powerful language, you've opened up a world of possibilities. However, as with any skill, continuous growth and exploration are essential to truly mastering Python and unlocking its full potential.

In this section, we'll explore various paths you can take to advance your Python knowledge and skills, helping you transition from a novice to a proficient and confident Python developer. Whether your goals lie in web development, data analysis, machine learning, or any other domain, this guide will provide you with a roadmap to navigate the vast Python ecosystem and continue your learning journey.

1. Practice, Practice, Practice

The age-old adage "practice makes perfect" rings true in the world of programming. Consistent practice is the key to solidifying your understanding of Python concepts and improving your coding skills. Here are some strategies to incorporate practice into your routine:

- **Code Along with Tutorials and Examples:** Seek out tutorials, coding challenges, and example projects that align with your interests. As you work through these resources, make sure to type out the code yourself rather than simply copying and pasting. This hands-on approach will reinforce your understanding and help you identify areas for improvement.

- **Build Personal Projects:** Identify a problem or idea that resonates with you and use Python to build a solution. Personal projects not only provide valuable practice opportunities but also allow you to apply your knowledge in a practical and meaningful way.

- **Participate in Online Coding Challenges:** Platforms like LeetCode, HackerRank, and CodeWars offer a vast collection of coding challenges ranging from beginner to advanced levels. Tackling these challenges will help you sharpen your problem-solving skills, expose you to different coding techniques, and provide a sense of accomplishment as you progress.

- **Contribute to Open-Source Projects:** The Python community embraces open-source development, and contributing to existing projects is an excellent way to gain practical experience, learn from experienced developers, and give back to the community. Start by identifying projects that align with your interests, review their contribution guidelines, and begin with small contributions like bug fixes or documentation improvements.

2. Explore Python Libraries and Frameworks

One of Python's greatest strengths lies in its extensive ecosystem of libraries and frameworks, which expand the language's capabilities and enable you to tackle a wide range of tasks and domains. Exploring and mastering these libraries and frameworks can greatly enhance your productivity and open up new opportunities. Here are some popular areas to consider:

- **Web Development:** Learn web development frameworks like Django and Flask to build robust and scalable web applications and APIs.

- **Data Analysis and Visualization:** Dive into libraries like NumPy, Pandas, and Matplotlib to analyze and visualize data, enabling you to uncover insights and make data-driven decisions.

- **Machine Learning and Deep Learning:** Explore libraries like scikit-learn, TensorFlow, and PyTorch to build and train machine learning models for tasks like image recognition, natural language processing, and predictive analytics.

- **Automation and Scripting:** Leverage libraries like Selenium and Requests to automate web interactions, scrape data from websites, and build powerful scripts for various tasks.

- **Game Development:** Explore game development libraries like Pygame and Arcade to create engaging and interactive games for desktop and mobile platforms.

As you delve into these libraries and frameworks, be sure to consult their official documentation, tutorials, and community resources for guidance and best practices.

3. Attend Workshops, Conferences, and Meetups

Networking and learning from experienced professionals can significantly accelerate your growth as a Python developer. Attending workshops, conferences, and local meetups provides valuable opportunities for hands-on learning, knowledge sharing, and connecting with the Python community.

- **Workshops:** Workshops are typically focused, intensive learning experiences led by experts in specific Python domains or technologies. These can range from introductory sessions to advanced workshops covering topics like web development, data analysis, or machine learning with Python.

- **Conferences:** Python conferences like PyCon, EuroPython, and PyData bring together Python enthusiasts, developers, and industry leaders from around the world. These events offer a diverse range of talks, tutorials, and networking opportunities, allowing you to stay up-to-date with the latest trends and best practices in the Python ecosystem.

- **Meetups:** Local Python meetups are great for connecting with fellow Python developers in your area, sharing knowledge and experiences, and learning about new tools and techniques. Many cities have active Python user groups that host regular meetups and presentations.

Attending these events not only enhances your technical skills but also provides opportunities for networking, finding mentors, and exploring potential job or collaboration opportunities within the Python community.

4. Pursue Online Courses and Certifications

The rise of online learning platforms has made it easier than ever to access high-quality educational resources and earn recognized certifications in Python and related technologies. Here are some options to consider:

- **Online Courses:** Platforms like Coursera, Udemy, and Pluralsight offer a wide range of Python courses taught by industry experts and experienced instructors. These courses cover various topics, from beginner-level Python programming to advanced subjects like data science, web development, and machine learning.

- **Specializations and Nanodegrees:** Several online learning platforms offer specialized programs or "nanodegrees" that provide comprehensive training and hands-on projects in specific Python domains, such as data analysis, machine learning, or full-stack web development.

- **Certifications:** Organizations like Python Institute and Certified Entry-Level Python Programmer (PCEP) offer professional certifications that validate your Python skills and knowledge. These certifications can be valuable additions to your resume and can demonstrate your proficiency to potential employers or clients.

When selecting online courses or certifications, be sure to research the instructors, course content, and reviews to ensure you're investing in high-quality educational resources that align with your learning goals.

5. Explore Domain-Specific Applications

While Python is a general-purpose programming language, it has found widespread adoption in various domains due to its versatility, readability, and extensive ecosystem of libraries and frameworks. Exploring domain-specific applications of Python can open up new career opportunities and deepen your understanding of how Python is used in real-world scenarios.

- **Scientific Computing and Research:** Python is widely used in scientific computing, data analysis, and research fields due to its powerful libraries like NumPy, SciPy, and Pandas. Learning how to leverage these tools can be valuable for roles in academia, research institutions, or data-driven organizations.

- **Web Development:** Python's web frameworks like Django and Flask have become popular choices for building robust and scalable web applications and APIs. Mastering these frameworks can lead to opportunities in web development, e-commerce, and software-as-a-service (SaaS) industries.

- **Data Analysis and Business Intelligence:** Python's data analysis and visualization capabilities make it an excellent choice for roles in data analysis, business intelligence, and data-driven decision-making. Libraries like Pandas, Matplotlib, and Seaborn can be powerful tools in these domains.

- **Machine Learning and Artificial Intelligence:** With its powerful machine learning and deep learning libraries like scikit-learn, TensorFlow, and PyTorch, Python has become a go-to language for building intelligent systems, predictive models, and AI applications.

- **Automation and Scripting:** Python's simplicity and readability make it an ideal choice for automating various tasks and processes, such as system administration, web scraping, and test automation. Mastering libraries like Selenium, Requests, and Paramiko can be valuable for roles in DevOps, automation, and software testing.

By exploring these domain-specific applications of Python, you can not only gain valuable skills and knowledge but also identify potential career paths that align with your interests and goals.

6. Stay Up-to-Date and Engage with the Community

The Python ecosystem is constantly evolving, with new libraries, frameworks, and best practices emerging regularly. Staying up-to-date and engaging with the Python community is essential to ensure that your skills remain relevant and to stay informed about the latest developments in the language and its applications.

- Follow Industry News and Blogs: Regularly read industry news, blogs, and publications focused on Python and software development. Sources like Python Insider, Real Python, and the official Python blogs can provide valuable insights and keep you informed about the latest trends and releases.

- Engage on Social Media: Join Python-related communities on social media platforms like Twitter, Reddit, and Discord. These platforms offer opportunities to connect with other Python enthusiasts, ask questions, and stay informed about upcoming events, job opportunities, and community initiatives.

- Contribute to Open-Source Projects: Python is an open-source language, and contributing to open-source projects can be a rewarding and educational experience. By reviewing code, fixing bugs, or adding new features, you can learn from experienced developers, gain practical experience, and contribute to the Python ecosystem.

- Attend Local Meetups and User Groups: Joining local Python meetups and user groups can provide valuable networking opportunities and hands-on learning experiences. These groups often host presentations, coding sessions, and discussions focused on various Python-related topics.

- Participate in Online Forums and Q&A Sites: Platforms like Stack Overflow, Python Forums, and the official Python mailing lists offer opportunities to ask questions, share knowledge, and learn from the collective wisdom of the Python community.

By actively engaging with the Python community, you'll not only stay informed about the latest developments but also gain access to a wealth of knowledge, support, and potential collaboration opportunities.

7. Pursue Personal Growth and Continuous Learning

Learning is a lifelong journey, and the pursuit of personal growth and continuous learning is essential for any aspiring Python developer. Here are some strategies to cultivate a growth mindset and embrace a culture of continuous learning:

- Read Books and Technical Publications: Explore books, technical publications, and online resources that cover a wide range of Python-related topics, from coding best practices and design patterns to domain-specific applications and emerging technologies.

- Learn from Mentors and Experienced Developers: Seek out mentors and experienced Python developers who can provide guidance, feedback, and insights based on their real-world experiences. Attending meetups, conferences, or joining online communities can help you connect with potential mentors.

- Experiment with New Technologies and Tools: Be open to exploring new technologies, libraries, and tools that complement your Python skills. This can help you stay ahead of the curve and expand your skillset, making you more adaptable and valuable in the ever-changing tech landscape.

- **Attend Workshops and Training Sessions:** Regularly attend workshops, training sessions, or online courses to learn new skills, update your knowledge, and stay current with the latest advancements in Python and related technologies.

- **Embrace Continuous Improvement:** Cultivate a mindset of continuous improvement by regularly reviewing your code, seeking feedback, and identifying areas for growth. Reflect on your experiences, learn from your mistakes, and strive to improve with each project or challenge you tackle.

By embracing personal growth and continuous learning, you'll not only enhance your Python skills but also develop a mindset that will serve you well throughout your career as a software developer.

Chapter 10: Appendices

10.1 Python Cheat Sheet

Python is a versatile and powerful programming language, but keeping track of all its syntax, functions, and features can be a daunting task, especially for beginners. That's where a Python cheat sheet comes in handy. A cheat sheet is a concise reference guide that provides a quick overview of the essential elements of a programming language, allowing you to quickly look up syntax, built-in functions, and other useful information.

In this section, we'll present a comprehensive Python cheat sheet that covers a wide range of topics, from basic data types and operators to more advanced concepts like object-oriented programming, file handling, and exception handling. Whether you're a beginner or an experienced Python programmer, this cheat sheet will serve as a valuable resource for quickly refreshing your memory or exploring new areas of the language.

Basic Syntax

```
# Single-line comment
"""
Multi-line comment
"""

print("Hello, World!")  # Output: Hello, World!
```

Data Types

Numbers

- int (e.g., 42, -3)
- float (e.g., 3.14, -0.5)
- complex (e.g., 3 + 4j)

Strings

- 'Single quotes'
- "Double quotes"
- """Triple quotes for multi-line strings"""

Booleans

- True
- False

Lists

- [1, 2, 3, 4, 5]
- ["apple", "banana", "cherry"]

Tuples

- (1, 2, 3)
- ("a", "b", "c")

Sets

- {1, 2, 3, 4, 5}

- {"apple", "banana", "cherry"}

Dictionaries

- {"name": "John", "age": 30}

Operators

Arithmetic Operators

- + (Addition)
- - (Subtraction)
- * (Multiplication)
- / (Division)
- % (Modulus)
- ** (Exponentiation)
- // (Floor Division)

Assignment Operators

- = (Assignment)
- += (Addition and Assignment)
- -= (Subtraction and Assignment)
- *= (Multiplication and Assignment)
- /= (Division and Assignment)
- %= (Modulus and Assignment)
- **= (Exponentiation and Assignment)
- //= (Floor Division and Assignment)

Comparison Operators

- == (Equal to)
- != (Not equal to)
- > (Greater than)
- < (Less than)
- >= (Greater than or equal to)
- <= (Less than or equal to)

Logical Operators

- and (Logical AND)
- or (Logical OR)
- not (Logical NOT)

Bitwise Operators

- & (Bitwise AND)
- | (Bitwise OR)
- ^ (Bitwise XOR)
- ~ (Bitwise NOT)
- << (Bitwise Left Shift)
- >> (Bitwise Right Shift)

Membership Operators

- in (Membership Test)
- not in (Non-Membership Test)

Identity Operators

- is (Identity Test)
- is not (Negated Identity Test)

Control Flow

If Statement

```python
if condition:
    # Code block
elif another_condition:
    # Code block
else:
    # Code block
```

For Loop

```python
for item in iterable:
    # Code block

for i in range(5):
    print(i)   # Output: 0 1 2 3 4
```

While Loop

```python
while condition:
    # Code block
```

Break and Continue

```python
for i in range(10):
    if i == 5:
        break  # Exits the loop
    if i % 2 == 0:
        continue  # Skips to the next iteration
    print(i)   # Output: 1 3
```

Functions

```python
def function_name(param1, param2, ...):
    """
    Docstring describing the function
    """
    # Function body
    return value
```

Object-Oriented Programming (OOP)

Classes

```python
class ClassName:
    """
    Docstring describing the class
    """
```

```python
    def __init__(self, param1, param2, ...):
        """
        Constructor method
        """
        self.attr1 = param1
        self.attr2 = param2

    def method_name(self, param):
        """
        Docstring describing the method
        """
        # Method body
```

Inheritance

```python
class DerivedClass(BaseClass):
    # Derived class implementation
```

File Handling

Reading a File

```python
with open("file.txt", "r") as file:
    content = file.read()
    print(content)
```

Writing to a File

```python
with open("file.txt", "w") as file:
    file.write("Hello, World!")
```

Exception Handling

```python
try:
    # Code that might raise an exception
except Exception as e:
    # Code to handle the exception
    print(e)
else:
    # Code to execute if no exception is raised
finally:
    # Code that will always be executed
```

Modules and Packages

Importing a Module

```python
import module_name
module_name.function()

from module_name import function
function()
```

Creating a Package

```python
package/
```

```
__init__.py
module1.py
module2.py
```

Python Style Guide (PEP 8)

- Use snake_case for function and variable names
- Use CamelCase for class names
- Use 4 spaces for indentation (no tabs)
- Follow maximum line length of 79 characters
- Use blank lines to separate logical blocks of code
- Include docstrings for modules, functions, classes, and methods

This Python cheat sheet covers the most essential concepts and syntax elements of the language. Keep it handy as a quick reference guide while coding, and use it as a starting point for exploring more advanced topics or refreshing your Python knowledge.

10.2 Additional Practice Problems

While the examples and exercises provided throughout this book are designed to reinforce your understanding of Python concepts, additional practice is always beneficial. In this section, we'll provide a collection of practice problems covering various topics, from basic data structures and control flow to more advanced concepts like object-oriented programming and file handling.

These practice problems are intended to challenge you and help you solidify your Python skills. Feel free to tackle them in any order, and don't hesitate to refer back to the relevant chapters or resources if you need a refresher. Remember, the more you practice, the more proficient you'll become in Python programming.

1. **Basic Data Types and Operations**
   - Write a program that takes two numbers as input and performs arithmetic operations (addition, subtraction, multiplication, and division) on them, displaying the results.
   - Create a program that generates a random password of a specified length, consisting of letters (both uppercase and lowercase), digits, and special characters.
   - Implement a function that takes a string as input and returns a reversed version of the string.
2. **Control Flow**
   - Write a program that takes a number as input and determines whether it is prime or not.
   - Create a program that generates the Fibonacci sequence up to a specified number of terms.
   - Implement a function that takes a list of numbers as input and returns the sum of all even numbers in the list.
3. **Data Structures**
   - Write a program that takes a sentence as input and returns a dictionary with the count of each word in the sentence.
   - Create a function that takes two lists as input and returns a new list containing the common elements between them.

- Implement a program that takes a list of numbers as input and returns a new list with all duplicate elements removed.

4. **Functions and Modules**
   - Write a function that takes a list of strings as input and returns a new list with all strings capitalized.
   - Create a module containing utility functions for working with strings (e.g., reverse a string, count vowels, remove punctuation).
   - Implement a function that takes a list of numbers as input and returns the sum of all numbers using recursion.

5. **File Handling**
   - Write a program that reads a text file and counts the number of lines, words, and characters in the file.
   - Create a program that takes a directory path as input and lists all files and subdirectories within that directory.
   - Implement a program that reads a CSV file and performs basic data analysis (e.g., calculating the mean, median, and mode of a specific column).

6. **Object-Oriented Programming (OOP)**
   - Design a class to represent a bank account, with methods for depositing, withdrawing, and checking the balance.
   - Create a class hierarchy for representing different types of vehicles (e.g., cars, trucks, motorcycles) with attributes and methods specific to each type.
   - Implement a class for representing a deck of cards, with methods for shuffling, dealing, and checking the remaining cards.

7. **Exception Handling**
   - Write a program that prompts the user to enter a file path and handles exceptions related to file operations (e.g., FileNotFoundError, PermissionError).
   - Create a function that takes a list of numbers as input and handles exceptions related to arithmetic operations (e.g., ZeroDivisionError, ValueError).
   - Implement a program that validates user input for various data types (e.g., integers, floats, strings) and handles exceptions related to invalid input.

8. **Advanced Topics**
   - Write a program that implements a simple web scraper to extract data from a website.
   - Create a command-line tool that interacts with a web API and displays the retrieved data in a user-friendly format.
   - Implement a program that reads and processes data from a database (e.g., SQLite, PostgreSQL, or MySQL) and generates a report or visualization based on the data.

These practice problems cover a wide range of topics and difficulty levels, ensuring that you can continuously challenge yourself and improve your Python skills. Remember to break down complex problems into smaller, manageable steps, and don't hesitate to seek help from online resources, documentation, or Python communities if you get stuck.

10.3 Glossary of Terms

As you delve deeper into Python programming, you'll encounter various terms and concepts that may be unfamiliar or confusing at first. To aid your understanding and provide a quick reference, we've compiled a glossary of common terms used in the Python ecosystem.

1. **Argument**: A value passed to a function or method when it is called. Arguments can be positional (ordered) or keyword (named).
2. **Attribute**: A characteristic or property associated with an object in Python. Attributes can be data values or methods.
3. **Built-in Function**: A function that is part of the Python language itself and is available for use without importing any additional modules.
4. **Class**: A blueprint or template for creating objects in object-oriented programming. Classes define the attributes and methods that objects of that class will have.
5. **Decorator**: A way to modify the behavior of a function or class without changing its source code directly.
6. **Docstring**: A string literal that serves as documentation for a module, function, class, or method, describing its purpose, parameters, and return values.
7. **Exception**: An error or exceptional condition that occurs during the execution of a program.
8. **Generator**: A special type of function that generates an iterator, which can be used to produce a sequence of values on-the-fly, saving memory compared to creating the entire sequence at once.
9. **Inheritance**: A mechanism in object-oriented programming where a new class (derived class) is based on an existing class (base class), inheriting its attributes and methods.
10. **Instance**: A specific object created from a class, with its own unique set of attribute values.
11. **Iterator**: An object that represents a stream of data, allowing you to access the next element in the stream using the next() function or a loop.
12. **Lambda Function**: A small, anonymous function that can be defined without a name, typically used for simple, one-line operations.
13. **List Comprehension**: A concise way to create a new list by applying an expression or transformation to each item in an existing iterable (e.g., list, tuple, or string).
14. **Method**: A function defined within a class and associated with objects of that class.
15. **Module**: A Python file containing definitions and statements, allowing you to organize and reuse code across multiple programs.
16. **Object**: An instance of a class, representing a specific entity or concept with its own set of attributes and methods.
17. **Package**: A collection of Python modules organized in a hierarchical directory structure, allowing for better code organization and modularization.
18. **Polymorphism**: The ability of objects of different classes to be treated as objects of a common superclass, enabling code reuse and flexibility.
19. **Python Interpreter**: The program that executes Python code by translating it into machine-readable instructions.
20. **Recursion**: A programming technique where a function calls itself to solve a problem by breaking it down into smaller instances of the same problem.
21. **Scope**: The region of a program where a variable or object is accessible and can be referenced.
22. **Sequence**: An ordered collection of items, such as a list, tuple, or string.
23. **Tuple**: An immutable sequence of values, similar to a list but enclosed in parentheses () instead of square brackets [].

24. **Type Hints**: Annotations in Python code that provide information about the expected types of variables, function parameters, and return values, helping with code readability and static type checking.
25. **Virtual Environment**: An isolated Python environment that allows you to install and manage packages and dependencies separately from your system's global Python installation.

This glossary covers some of the most common terms you'll encounter in the world of Python programming. As you continue to explore and work with Python, you'll likely come across additional terms and concepts. Don't hesitate to refer back to this glossary or consult other resources to expand your understanding of Python's terminology and concepts.